# ILTS Early Childhood Special Education (152) Exam

"You never fail until you stop trying" - Albert Einstein

For inquiries;
info@xmprep.com

Unauthorised copying of any part of this test is illegal.

# ILTS Early Childhood Special Education (152) Exam #1

## Test Taking Tips

☐ Take a deep breath and relax

☐ Read directions carefully

☐ Read the questions thoroughly

☐ Make sure you understand what is being asked

☐ Go over all of the choices before you answer

☐ Paraphrase the question

☐ Eliminate the options you know are wrong

☐ Check your work

☐ Think positively and do your best

## Table of Contents

| SECTION 1 | |
|---|---|
| DIRECTION | 1 |
| PRACTICE TEST | 2 - 20 |
| ANSWER KEY | 21 |
| SECTION 2 | |
| DIRECTION | 22 |
| PRACTICE TEST | 23 - 39 |
| ANSWER KEY | 40 |
| SECTION 3 | |
| DIRECTION | 41 |
| PRACTICE TEST | 42 - 57 |
| ANSWER KEY | 58 |
| SECTION 4 | |
| DIRECTION | 59 |
| PRACTICE TEST | 60 - 74 |
| ANSWER KEY | 75 |
| SECTION 5 | |
| DIRECTION | 76 |
| PRACTICE TEST | 77 - 89 |
| ANSWER KEY | 90 |
| SECTION 6 | |
| DIRECTION | 91 |
| PRACTICE TEST | 92 - 106 |
| ANSWER KEY | 107 |

Copyright © Educational Testing Group, All rights reserved.
This booklet may not be reproduced and transmitted in any form by any means without the permission of the publisher.
This booklet has been prepared and printed in USA.

# TEST DIRECTION

**DIRECTIONS**

Read the questions carefully and then choose the ONE best answer to each question.

Be sure to allocate your time carefully so you are able to complete the entire test within the testing session. You may go back and review your answers at any time.

You may use any available space in your test booklet for scratch work.

Questions in this booklet are not actual test questions but they are the samples for commonly asked questions.

This test aims to cover all topics which may appear on the actual test. However some topics may not be covered.

Studying this booklet will be preparing you for the actual test. It will not guarantee improving your test score but it will help you pass your exam on the first attempt.

**Some useful tips for answering multiple choice questions;**

- Start with the questions that you can easily answer.

- Underline the keywords in the question.

- Be sure to read all the choices given.

- Watch for keywords such as NOT, always, only, all, never, completely.

- Do not forget to answer every question.

**1**

The use of modeling technique is most appropriate in which elements of a lesson plan?

A) Opening
B) Student practice
C) Introduction of new material
D) All of the above

**2**

Early intervention services are provided under the Individuals with Disabilities Education Act (IDEA). Through grants to each state from the federal government, children who qualify may receive services free of charge or at low cost.

Which of the following age ranges are children qualified for the program?

A) 7-8 years
B) 5-6 years
C) 3-4 years
D) 0-3 years

**3**

Which of the following best describes a responsibility of a paraeducator in a general education classroom that includes several students with the learning disability?

A) Assisting the students with learning disabilities during small-group instruction
B) Scheduling related support services for the students with learning disabilities
C) Planning weekly lessons and activities for the entire class
D) Administering formal classroom assessments to the entire class

**4**

Neil, a high school student with a learning disability, has been suspended for ten days and requested for a meeting since he is skipping classes, disrespecting teachers and fighting in class.

Which of the following should an IEP team do next to Neil's case?

A) Eligibility determination meeting
B) Standardized achievement test
C) Functional behavior assessment
D) Due process hearing

**5**

A 9-year old boy is observed to have difficulty completing tasks in school because of lack of focus and impulsive behaviors. However, his intelligence and achievement test scores fall in average for his age.

Which of the following diagnosis is his symptoms match?

A) Attention-deficit/hyperactivity disorder (ADHD)
B) Specific learning disability (SLD)
C) Oppositional defiant disorder (ODD)
D) Traumatic brain injury (TBI)

**6**

A special education teacher observes a 4-year-old preschooler who demonstrates repetitive motor behaviors such as hand flapping and spinning that interfere with the classroom routine and the child's ability to play. The teacher records the observations and notices they consistently occur when he is asked to transition from one activity to another.

Which of the following can be used to describe the transition times in relation to the identified behaviors?

A) Consequences
B) Interventions
C) Antecedents
D) Reinforcers

**7**

Which of the following is a sign of having an Attention-deficit disorder, ADD?

A) Delay in fine and motor skills
B) Difficulty in expressing oneself verbally
C) Difficulty in performing strenuous activities
D) Lack of impulse control

**8**

**The Individuals with Disabilities Education Act (IDEA)** is a four-part (A-D) piece of American legislation that ensures students with a disability are provided with Free Appropriate Public Education (FAPE) that is tailored to their individual needs.

Which of the following does least restrictive environment (LPE) suggest to students with a disability as defined in IDEA?

A) Educate with the most assistance, whether or not it be in the same environment as with nondisabled peers
B) Educate in a particular school so that there is no interaction with nondisabled peers
C) Educate with nondisabled peers to the most significant extent possible
D) Educate with nondisabled peers only for elective courses

**9**

Pete exhibits inappropriate responses and mood swings. He also begins to start fights in school and act out of class.

What do you call this kind of disorder?

A) ADD
B) Mental Retardation
C) Emotional Disturbance
D) Huntington's Disease

**10**

Which of the following aspects of communication development is likely to be most difficult for a student who has an emotional behavioral disability?

A) Interpreting a speaker's feelings from his or her tone of voice
B) Producing fluent speech that is free of articulation errors
C) Understanding new vocabulary words in context
D) Using syntax patterns that are grammatically correct

**11**

Which of the following is significantly more challenging for a young child with a visual impairment?

A) Develop a sense of identity
B) Acquire incidental information from the environment
C) Maintain positive peer relationships
D) Comprehend concrete concepts through direct instruction

**12**

Which of the following should be the focus of an IEP team that is planning transition for a student with a disability?

A) Selecting the most appropriate diploma option for the student
B) Conducting a suitability assessment for postsecondary options
C) Providing opportunities for the student to engage in job shadowing
D) Ensuring that a person-centered approach is used

**13**

Summative assessments are used to evaluate student learning, skill acquisition, and academic achievement.

Which of the following illustrates a summative assessment?

A) Completing a homework assignment
B) Practicing how to write the directions for baking a cake
C) An end of chapter test
D) Writing sentences using spelling words

**14**

Earl, a sixth-grade student with a specific learning disability in mathematics computation, is independent most of the time in completing classroom assignments.

Which of the following strategies should the teacher use to increase Earl's independence in doing his work if he has been successfully modeling and prompting the student during the instruction?

A) Fading
B) Punishment
C) Extinction
D) Ignoring

**15**

Lead is a neurotoxic substance that has been shown in numerous research studies to affect brain function and development. Children who have been exposed to elevated levels of lead are at increased risk for cognitive and behavioral problems during development.

Which of the following conditions would a young child exposed to high levels of lead most likely develop?

A) Type 2 diabetes
B) Visual impairment
C) Severe food allergies
D) Impaired cognitive skills

**16**

The basis for a positive behavioral support program for all students, including students with special needs being implemented in an elementary school has its foundation in which of the following principles of behavior theory?

A) Modeling
B) Extinction
C) Reinforcement
D) Shaping

**17**

Which of the following fine-motor skills do children usually develop last according to typical physical development?

A) Stringing large beads
B) Buttoning large buttons
C) Stacking and building with blocks
D) Copying circles and crosses with crayons

**18**

A student with a cognitive impairment shows several academic regression during school breaks which may lead to the student to experience significant setbacks over summer vacation.

Which of the following would be best for the teacher to advocate the student?

A) Referring the student's parents or guardians to tutors they could engage to work with their child in the summer.
B) Meeting with the student's assigned teacher for the next year to recommend ways to help the student make up for lost ground.
C) Providing the student's family with materials and activities designed to help the student maintain the skills learned in the current year.
D) Making a recommendation that the student receives extended educational services during the upcoming summer.

**19**

**A specific learning disability (SLD)** is a disorder in one or more of the fundamental psychological processes involved in understanding or in using language, spoken or written.

The class lesson for the day is about solving addition problems. However, one of the students has a specific learning disability (SLD) in Math. For his individualized education program (IEP), which of the following should be included?

A) Reading problems to him during tests
B) Permitting him to use a calculator to solve word problems
C) Allowing him to answer word problems verbally during tests
D) Allowing him to use manipulatives to solve word problems

**20**

What genetic disorder is illustrated by the existence of an extra copy of genetic material on chromosome 21?

A) Down syndrome
B) Tourette syndrome
C) Hungtinton's disease
D) Multiple Sclerosis

**21**

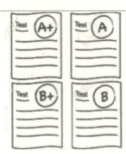

Which of the following should Mr.Adam do to his student who showed a great performance in improving his academics?

A) Give the student higher levels of work
B) Reward the student by excusing them from assignments
C) Call home and praise the student's progress
D) Hold an IEP to discuss options for a less restrictive environment

**22**

For behavioral issues in the classroom, which of the following shows the least biased intervention?

A) Giving a student a lunch detention for speaking without raising their hand in class
B) Explaining to students what their behaviors should look like and creating class norms with the students
C) Class suspensions for acts of defiance
D) Creating a system of rewards and consequences that addresses standard behaviors

**23**

In the monthly group meetings for students' parents or guardians held by an elementary special education teacher, several parents or guardians asked for ways for them to support their child's learning at home.

Which guideline would be the most critical to keep in mind for a teacher involving the development of suggestions for the parents or guardians?

A) Each task should be accompanied by a simple way to measure and document progress.
B) Activities should provide remedial practice in skills that students are learning at school.
C) Each task should be designed so that the families will need to work together for several weeks to complete it.
D) Activities should be meaningful and should fit comfortably into the family's daily schedule.

**24**

A stanine score is a way to scale scores on a nine-point scale. Which of the following mathematics classes is most appropriate for a seventh-grade student with a specific learning disability and a stanine score of 9 in mathematics?

A) Standard mathematics
B) Advanced mathematics
C) Functional mathematics
D) Remedial mathematics

**25**

What assessment procedures should the teacher use to monitor the students' progress toward their Individualized Education Program (IEP) goals related to enhancing word vocabulary and fluency?

A) Administering an informal reading inventory to each student on a monthly basis
B) Developing individual portfolios in which each student collects a list of mastered sight words every week
C) Conducting an error analysis of each student's oral reading on a monthly basis
D) Reviewing data on each students reading accuracy and speed on a graph every week

**26**

An **Individual Family Service Plan (IFSP)** is a plan for special services for young children with developmental delays.

Which of the following would be included in an Individualized Family Service Plan (IFSP) for a 2-year-old child under the provisions of IDEA?

A) A recommendation of counseling for the child's siblings
B) Techniques for the family to use in introducing academic subjects
C) A budget for early-intervention services
D) Plans for making the transition into preschool

**27**

In order to help students build their confidence in reading, which of the following techniques would best help Ms. Edwards introduce cultural traditions around the world through a short story?

A) Having students write summaries of their own cultural traditions

B) Assigning different students different stories to read and summarize for the rest of the class

C) Comparing and contrasting different cultures

D) Activating prior knowledge by asking students about their own family/cultural traditions

**28**

Which of the following would be an appropriate accommodation for Sally's Gen-ed teacher to make given that she is diagnosed with a Specific Learning Disability who struggles with math?

A) Excusing the student from all math assignments

B) Providing the student with 3rd-grade math work

C) Allowing the student to complete only evens or odds on a math worksheet

D) Allowing the student to complete the assignment using a calculator

**29**

**Least Restrictive Environment (LRE)** is the requirement in federal law that students with disabilities receive their education, to the maximum extent appropriate, with nondisabled peers and that special education students are not removed from regular classes unless, even with supplemental aids and services, education in regular classes cannot be achieved satisfactorily.

According to LRE which would be the most appropriate setting to start in for Dottie, 8-year-old, who qualifies IEP under Emotionally Disturbed and has had several behavioral issues around assaulting students and adults?

A) Separate Day School
B) Separate Day Class
C) Resource pull out services twice a day
D) Inclusion program

**30**

Which collaborative approach would likely be most useful for the teacher to use in facilitating Individualized Education Program (IEP) team meetings involving numerous service providers within the school and community?

A) Monitoring team members interactions carefully to minimize the conflicts
B) Assigning specific tasks to each team member to complete before each meeting
C) Organizing meetings so that each member has a set time limit for presenting information to the team
D) Listening actively to clarify and summarize team members input during discussions

**31**

During the designing of a mathematics learning center of a kindergarten class, a general education teacher suggests materials that a special education teacher who co-teaches feels may not be very accessible to disabled students.

Which of the following strategies should the special education teacher take to promote communication and collaboration between the two of them?

A) Agree to use the materials but insist that disable students will be given extra support with them.
B) Request for a space in the learning center dedicated to disabled students with materials especially for them.
C) Use research articles about disabled students to voice her opinion about the materials that will be used.
D) Point out specific aspects of the materials that would be challenging and suggest possible alternative materials to be used for disabled students.

**32**

For a student suspected of having a specific learning disability, which of the following is legally required in initiating a formal evaluation?

A) Signed parental permission
B) Physician referral
C) The verbal agreement provided by the parents
D) Teacher referral

**33**

In an elementary school special education classroom, what practice will best prevent the spread of illnesses such as common cold and flu?

A) Encouraging students not to bring in food from home to share with classmates.
B) Providing students with individual boxes of tissues to keep at their personal belongings.
C) Assigning students a specific area in the classroom for storing their personal belongings.
D) Having students wash their hands properly on a regular basis throughout the day.

**34**

**Self-determination** refers to the characteristic of a person that leads them to make choices and decisions based on their preferences and interests.

Which of the following should the curriculum of a high school ESE class focus on to improve the students' self-determination skills?

A) Teaching students strategies to achieve their desired goals.
B) Teaching students how to use adaptive technology in their home environments.
C) Helping students understand laws related to individuals with disabilities.
D) Helping students understand the benefits of living independently after high school.

**35**

Which of the following do students with learning disabilities possess rather than students without disabilities?

A) Selective attention disorders
B) Deficits in long-term memory retrieval
C) Characteristics of giftedness in artistic expression
D) Clear dominance of the left brain for learning

**36**

A 5-year-old boy is diagnosed with a developmental delay. Which of the following symptoms is most likely shown?

A) He tends to be closer to most adults than his peers.
B) He is having difficulties while reading.
C) He avoids eye contact with others.
D) He is unable to distinguish specific colors.

**37**

You have a student named John, with Down syndrome. How can you help him push through the class if other students are making fun of him?

A) Send the involved students to the guidance counselor's office
B) Advocate a "No-Bully" campaign
C) Have a conference with the parents of the students involved
D) Advice John to transfer to another school

**38**

Ariel is in Grade 2 and he was diagnosed with Down syndrome. At home, he was bound to some regulations and limitations by his parents but his teacher is complaining about his disobedience to simple rules inside the classroom.

Which is the most suitable way to deal with this problem?

A) Strategize with his parents on how they can begin to hold him to higher expectations.
B) Begin to lower your expectations on Ariel.
C) Take away Ariel's play time until such time he meets your expectations.
D) Strategize with her parents to be able to point out the ways they allowed his misbehaviors.

**39**

Which of the following could be the best method for a particular educator to help a middle school student with specific learning disabilities to his Individualized Education Program (IEP) goal in developing self-determination skills?

A) Providing the student with reading material to learn more about the IEP process
B) Providing the student with opportunities to evaluate his work
C) Providing the student with opportunities to evaluate his work
D) Including the student as a collaborator at his own IEP annual review meeting

**40**

Which of the following would be the most appropriate classroom setting for Miguel, an 8th-grade student, who has a specific learning disability in the area of math?

A) An after-school math tutoring program
B) A special day class where he attends math and science and is mainstreamed for his other classes
C) A resource program that provides push in/pull out for math and allows him to remain in the gen-ed setting
D) A non-public school for students with SLD's

CONTINUE ▶

**41**

A parent has addressed to the ESE (Exceptional Student Education) teacher his concern that his son always comes home crying and saying that no one likes him.

How would the ESE teacher respond to the parent?

A) Paraphrasing the parent's statement and soliciting further information about the situation
B) Providing the parent with the telephone number of a local mental health agency
C) Assuring the parent that every student has a difficult day now and then
D) Expressing sympathy to the parent and then redirecting the discussion to the planned agenda

**42**

**Autism Spectrum Disorder (ASD)** is a lifelong developmental disability that affects, among other things, the way an individual relates to his or her environment.

During class, a fourth-grade student with ASD has been observed to have difficulty maintaining eye contact and makes impulsive comments.

Which of the following would be the best approach in dealing with his behavior?

A) Provide a visual menu of appropriate behaviors
B) Give high-interest, low-reading-level assignments
C) Assign a peer buddy to help him keep on task
D) Seat next to the window so he can look outside

**43**

**Co-teaching** is a model that emphasizes collaboration and communication among all members of a team to meet the needs of all students.

If the lead and support teachers each deliver a lesson to a separate group of students, which of the following would be the most effective teaching?

A) Alternative teaching
B) Parallel teaching
C) Shared teaching
D) Complementary teaching

**44**

A person with a mild intellectual disability will have a significant difficulty managing his life effectively without support and training.

Before a behavior intervention plan (BIP), which of the following should be done?

A) Applying the current behavior reward system
B) Hiring a paraprofessional to work with him
C) Conducting a functional behavioral assessment
D) Assigning homework less frequently

**45**

Ms. Ella is an elementary ESE teacher having a student with a specific learning disability in Mathematics. She collects her student's homework and classroom assignments twice a week to gather data.

For which of the following could the data be useful?

A) Assessing the student's learning aptitude
B) Evaluating the student's ability to participate in statewide testing
C) Assigning the student a report card grade
D) Monitoring student progress and the effectiveness of instruction

**46**

To promote successful use of assistive technology, a fifth-grade student with specific learning disability receives an assignment including the use of word processing and speech recognition software.

Which of the following is the most effective method for the student to be familiarized with the technology?

A) Providing software for home use
B) Allowing choice of topic for written assignments
C) Limiting the amount of written homework
D) Assigning keyboarding homework

**47**

Which of the following steps would be most useful for a new middle school teacher to take when preparing for his initial meeting with an experienced paraeducator who will assist him in providing services to students in the special education program?

A) Asking the paraeducator to provide a resume and other documentation of previous work experience
B) Asking other teachers who have worked with her to give him anecdotal information about the paraeducator
C) Compiling a comprehensive list of program needs and tasks that the paraeducator must complete
D) Familiarizing himself with the defined roles and expectations for paraeducators in his district

**48**

Which of the following describes an educational approach from which elementary students with moderate intellectual disabilities would typically benefit most?

A) An educational approach that promotes daily living skills through drill and practice
B) An educational approach that focuses primarily on guided discovery learning
C) An educational approach that integrates a functional curriculum with hands-on community-based learning
D) An educational approach that waves creative visual and performing arts activities throughout the curriculum

**49**

A student who is an English Language Learner (ELL) may have a mild intellectual disability.

Which of the following could help a teacher confirm that intellectual disability is unrelated to being bilingual and to second-language acquisition issues?

A) By asking a colleague who is well versed in special education and ESL instruction to review the evaluation procedures for possible bias.

B) By using informal assessment procedures and instruments rather than formal standardized methods and tools to evaluate the student.

C) By recommending that the student is reevaluated using a different bilingual assessor and comparing the results of the two evaluations.

D) By meeting with the student's parents/guardians and an interpreter to inquire about the student's behaviors and abilities outside of school.

**50**

In fostering self-advocacy and independence in children who have mild to moderate intellectual disabilities, which of the following factors has the most significant influence?

A) Establishing friendships with peers both with and without special needs

B) Becoming a member of an advocacy group for individuals with disabilities

C) Receiving positive support from parents/guardians who believe in their potential

D) Obtaining instruction in inclusive settings with experienced educators

**51**

Eliza has a moderate traumatic brain injury. She received speech-language, physical, and occupational therapies and had an Individualized Education Program (IEP).

Which of the following best describes the educational implications of Eliza's disease?

A) Eliza's condition will prevent her from taking college preparation classes.
B) Eliza's academic course load should be modified or reduced as she transitions back into the school environment.
C) Eliza will likely require speech-language, physical, and occupational therapies for the remainder of high school.
D) Eliza will likely require instructional services at home in addition to those she receives at school.

**52**

To demonstrate a student has reached Bloom's Skill level of Synthesis, which of the following would be an appropriate objective?

A) Students analyze multiple step linear equations.
B) Student solves multiple step linear equations.
C) Student recognizes multiple step linear equations.
D) Students formulate multiple step linear equations.

## SECTION 1

| # | Answer | Topic | Subtopic | # | Answer | Topic | Subtopic | # | Answer | Topic | Subtopic | # | Answer | Topic | Subtopic |
|---|---|---|---|---|---|---|---|---|---|---|---|---|---|---|---|
| 1 | D | TB | SB2 | 14 | A | TB | SB2 | 27 | B | TB | SB2 | 40 | C | TB | SB2 |
| 2 | D | TA | SA2 | 15 | D | TA | SA1 | 28 | D | TB | SB2 | 41 | A | TB | SB1 |
| 3 | A | TB | SB2 | 16 | C | TA | SA1 | 29 | C | TA | SA2 | 42 | A | TA | SA1 |
| 4 | C | TA | SA2 | 17 | B | TA | SA1 | 30 | D | TA | SA2 | 43 | B | TB | SB1 |
| 5 | A | TA | SA1 | 18 | D | TB | SB1 | 31 | D | TB | SB2 | 44 | C | TA | SA1 |
| 6 | C | TB | SB2 | 19 | D | TA | SA2 | 32 | A | TB | SB2 | 45 | D | TB | SB2 |
| 7 | D | TA | SA1 | 20 | A | TA | SA1 | 33 | D | TB | SB2 | 46 | A | TB | SB2 |
| 8 | C | TA | SA2 | 21 | D | TB | SB2 | 34 | A | TB | SB2 | 47 | D | TB | SB1 |
| 9 | C | TA | SA1 | 22 | B | TB | SB2 | 35 | A | TA | SA1 | 48 | C | TB | SB2 |
| 10 | A | TB | SB1 | 23 | D | TB | SB1 | 36 | C | TA | SA1 | 49 | D | TA | SA2 |
| 11 | B | TA | SA1 | 24 | B | TB | SB2 | 37 | B | TB | SB2 | 50 | C | TA | SA1 |
| 12 | D | TA | SA2 | 25 | D | TA | SA2 | 38 | A | TB | SB1 | 51 | B | TA | SA2 |
| 13 | C | TB | SB2 | 26 | D | TA | SA2 | 39 | D | TA | SA2 | 52 | D | TB | SB2 |

## Topics & Subtopics

| Code | Description | Code | Description |
|---|---|---|---|
| SA1 | Understanding Disabilities | SB2 | Instructional Strategies |
| SA2 | Individualized Education Plan (IEP) | TA | Disabilities |
| SB1 | Collaboration & Communication | TB | Learning Environment |

# TEST DIRECTION

**DIRECTIONS**

Read the questions carefully and then choose the ONE best answer to each question.

Be sure to allocate your time carefully so you are able to complete the entire test within the testing session. You may go back and review your answers at any time.

You may use any available space in your test booklet for scratch work.

Questions in this booklet are not actual test questions but they are the samples for commonly asked questions.

This test aims to cover all topics which may appear on the actual test. However some topics may not be covered.

Studying this booklet will be preparing you for the actual test. It will not guarantee improving your test score but it will help you pass your exam on the first attempt.

**Some useful tips for answering multiple choice questions;**

- Start with the questions that you can easily answer.

- Underline the keywords in the question.

- Be sure to read all the choices given.

- Watch for keywords such as NOT, always, only, all, never, completely.

- Do not forget to answer every question.

**1**

Emmanuel has a cochlear implant disorder. His family is ashamed of having him around whether they go out in public or just at home.

What kind of an impact might this have on Emmanuel's development?

A) No impact at all
B) He will separate himself from his family and try to find comfort in his peers
C) Negative impact on his self-confidence
D) Both B and C

**2**

Which of the following data collection tools would be most appropriate for a special education teacher to use when she plans to conduct a weekly home visit to observe a 10-month-old child who has Down syndrome?

A) Criterion-referenced measures
B) Readiness assessment
C) Informal parent interview
D) Developmental checklist

**3**

Brent, a sixth-grade student with autism spectrum disorder (ASD), attends a full-time general education class along with his special education teacher.

To integrate social skills with academic curricula, which of the following would be the best strategy for the Individualized Education Program (IEP) team?

A) Assign the student a one-on-one aide to model appropriate behavior.
B) Include peer-to-peer supports in the general education class as part of the student's IEP.
C) Establish clear expectations for appropriate classroom behavior.
D) Incorporate individual counseling services into the student's IEP.

**4**

Which of the following is to be achieved in following established basal and ceiling levels when administering a standardized achievement test?

A) Develop the student's individualized instructional objectives
B) Determine the student's grade equivalency
C) Rank the student's abilities among peers
D) Focus on the student's specific range of academic skills

**5**

Which of the following statements shows a required component that must be found in the Individual Family Service Plan (IFSP) of a toddler?

A) A summary of the research that supports the interventions that will be implemented with the child.
B) A description of the qualifications of specialists and other professionals who will be working with the child.
C) A statement of the family's resources, priorities, and concerns relating to enhancing the child's development.
D) A list of any known genetic or environmental factors that may be relevant to the child's disability.

**6**

It is a disorder that affects muscle tone, movement, and motor skills caused by brain damage that happens before or during a baby's birth, or during the first 3 to 5 years of a child's life.

Which of the following disorder is defined above?

A) Cystic fibrosis
B) Muscular dystrophy
C) Cerebral palsy
D) Multiple sclerosis

**7**

The Individuals with Disabilities Education Improvement Act (IDEA) provides students with disabilities some procedural safeguards to protect their rights.

Which of the following does IDEA require before evaluating a student for special education services?

A) An independent psychologist must review the referral information and determine that an evaluation is necessary.
B) The student's parents/guardians must give written permission for the evaluation.
C) A school administrator must allocate funding for the evaluation to take place.
D) The student's general education teacher must submit a list of assessments to include in the evaluation.

**8**

Ms. Sheena is the mother of a nonverbal child, Ana. Which of the following should a teacher tell Ms. Sheena to give functional language training to Ana?

A) Teaching the child to point to the sink when she wants a drink of water
B) Drilling on bilabial sounds so the child can say "mama"
C) Rewarding the child for making a vocalization approximating a sound made by Ms. Ana
D) Rewarding the child for any vocalization made while looking at Ms. Ana

**9**

Which of the following abilities emerge first according to typical childhood motor development?

A) Doing a series of forwarding rolls
B) Descending the stairs using alternating feet
C) Running in one direction smoothly
D) Hopping forward on one foot at least ten times

**10**

Which of the following instruction is an ESE (Exceptional Student Education) teacher demonstrating if he uses different learning styles to address the diverse learning strengths and challenges of every student?

A) Performance-based instruction
B) Direct instruction
C) Computer-based instruction
D) Differentiated instruction

**11**

Mica is a 10-year-old student with an intellectual disability to retain previously acquired skills.

Which of the following would help to improve her learning?

A) Acknowledging appropriate behavior regularly
B) Scheduling frequent peer tutoring sessions
C) Allowing longer independent practice periods
D) Providing periodic review of lessons

**12**

Which of the following procedures must an Individualized Education Program (IEP) team follow to determine a student's eligibility for special education services?

A) Documenting the student's aptitude based on standardized achievement instruments
B) Evaluating the students in all areas of suspected disability
C) Evaluating the students adaptive functioning abilities with behavioral rating scales
D) Administering formal instrument to obtain a standardized score

**13**

A high school teacher likes to improve his students with learning disabilities in the content area reading comprehension.

Which of the following would be most helpful to use?

A) Graphic organizer
B) Word list
C) Storyboard
D) Basal reader

**14**

Which of the following must any IEP meet IDEA's requirements for function?

A) The IEP must be in effect before special education services, or related services are provided
B) The IEP must not be made available to any school personnel except special education teachers
C) The IEP must include a multiyear outline of instructional objectives
D) The IEP must include a section on assistive devices, regardless of the nature or degree of the student's disability

**15**

Rewards are given in recognition of one's efforts or achievements. Third-grade students show exemplary behavior in class. Which of the following would be the most appropriate reward for them?

A) Excusing them from the next chapter test
B) Providing extra computer time
C) Giving them ice-cream sandwiches as an afternoon treat
D) Assigning no homework for an entire week

**16**

Which of the following type of intelligence does Mario, a student with an IEP, benefit most from lectures and written assignments?

A) Linguistic Intelligence
B) Intrapersonal Intelligence
C) Spatial Intelligence
D) Logical-Mathematical

**17**

For an eight-year-old student with a mild intellectual disability, what activity would he/she find most difficult?

A) Recognizing the letters within his or her first time
B) Following basic two-step oral directions
C) Using a previously learned skill in a new setting
D) Matching two similar objects together

**18**

**The syntax** is the grammar, structure, or order of the elements in a language statement.

Andre frequently uses inappropriate syntax. Which of the following is an example?

A) Saying, "Wa wa" as a substitute for water
B) Saying, "He drinked his milk"
C) Saying, "I see football game"
D) Saying, "Me sister shoes new happy"

**19**

A special education teacher noticed that a fifth-grade general education teacher he has collaborated with does not involve students with disabilities in class activities.

Which of the following steps should the special education teacher take first to address this issue?

A) Discuss the concerns with the general education teacher.
B) Convene the students' Individualized Education Program (IEP) teams to discuss the change in placement.
C) Ask the school psychologist to observe in the classroom.
D) Report the general education teacher's behavior to the administrator.

**20**

Which of the following is an American non-profit professional organization concerned with publishing a definition and classification manual that emphasizes systems of support for individuals with intellectual disabilities?

A) The Arc of the United States
B) The American Association on Intellectual and Developmental Disabilities
C) Autism Society of America
D) National Down Syndrome Congress

CONTINUE ▶

**21**

Which of the following is most likely to promote successful use of assistive technology for students such as Jen, a 6th-grade student, who receives special education services under the category of specific learning disability?

A) Allowing choice of topic for written assignments
B) Providing software for home use
C) Limiting the amount or written homework
D) Increasing the amount or written homework

**22**

A middle school student has autism spectrum disorder (ASD). It is a lifelong developmental disability that affects, among other things, the way an individual relates to his or her environment.

Which of the following would support him to be successful in his schooling?

A) Taking him on a tour of the school so that she can become familiar with the layout of the classrooms
B) Providing him with time away from her classmates when she has an outburst
C) Providing him with a visual schedule of daily activities
D) Allowing him to attend school for a half-day for the first month

**23**

When conflicts arise during unstructured playtime in a prekindergarten inclusion setting, which of the following is the primary role of the teacher?

A) Help children develop appropriate ways to resolve the conflict.
B) Intervene and discipline children as soon as conflict occurs during activity.
C) Reconsider the need for free play in the prekindergarten schedule.
D) Teach children the essential features of good manners and etiquette.

**24**

The rights and full participation of children and adults with intellectual and developmental disabilities have been advocated by which of the following organizations?

A) Council for Exceptional Children
B) Project HOPE
C) The Arc of the United States
D) Make-A-Wish Foundation

**25**

A special education teacher acting as a service coordinator suggests to the Individual Family Service Plan (ISFP) team to engage the parents of a 3-year-old child with fetal alcohol syndrome (FAS) as collaborative partners in developing a transition plan for the child as he enters a public preschool.

Which of the following strategies would be most useful to use to accomplish this goal?

A) Suggest that the parents observe and take notes about the transition planning process during the first meeting.
B) Refer the parents to online and print resources that offer general information about the transition planning process.
C) Ask the parents to provide information to the team members that would help them understand the family's concerns, resources, and priorities.
D) Encourage the parents to write down comments and concerns for the teacher so that she could share them with the members of the team.

**26**

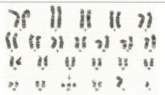

**Trisomy 21** is a genetic disorder caused by the presence of all or part of the third copy of chromosome 21.

Which of the following is another name given to Trisomy 21?

A) Turner Syndrome
B) Klinefelter Syndrome
C) Down Syndrome
D) Phenylketonuria (PKU)

27

Which of the following questions would be most important for an IEP team to focus on during the review of a recently drafted IEP for a middle school student with autism spectrum disorder (ASD) and associated intellectual disability?

A) Is current research supporting significant components of the student's IEP cited within the document?
B) Is the IEP sufficiently broad and inclusive to remain in effect until the student's reevaluation in three years?
C) Does the IEP distinguish between the student's academic and social needs?
D) Does the IEP provide a detailed outline of what the student needs to access and make progress in the general education curriculum?

28

A student is observed to be diligent and often have short pauses and repetition of words when excited.

What is the most indicative observation for a student to be referred to a speech-language pathologist for an evaluation?

A) The student's disfluencies often occur when he speaks at a faster rate than he usually talks.
B) The student is more disfluent with specific types of words, such as new vocabulary and compound words.
C) The student's speech tends to include more disfluencies at the end of the day than at the beginning.
D) The student demonstrates other behaviors, such as eye blinking or throat clearing, when he is disfluent.

### 29

Which of the following placements would be most appropriate for Jodeen, a 7-year-old with mild expressive language delay, given that her hearing and functioning in all areas is normal?

A) A part-time placement in a resource room for developmental and oral reading
B) A full-time general education placement with an emphasis on reading support
C) A full-time general education placement with speech and language services
D) A self-contained special education class with speech and language services

### 30

**Dyscalculia** is a specific developmental disorder that is characterized difficulty in learning or comprehending arithmetic.

With which of the following tasks would a third-grade student with dyscalculia likely have the most difficulty?

A) Copying a word from the class word wall to use in a story
B) Cutting out pictures from magazines to create a collage
C) Playing a game involving quantity and place value
D) Saying a word that rhymes with a word stated by the teacher

### 31

Which of the following would be the most effective regarding a student with attention-deficit/hyperactivity disorder (ADHD) having difficulty in starting a long-term writing assignment?

A) Asking the library media specialist to research and locate information for the student on her assigned writing topic.
B) Working with the student and the English language arts teacher to break down the assignment into smaller, more manageable parts.
C) Scheduling a meeting with the student and her parents to discuss her negative attitude toward the assignment.
D) Suggesting that the English language arts teacher provide the student with a different topic for the writing assignment.

### 32

Which of the following is guaranteed in the rights of students to be eligible for ESE, exceptional student education, services according to the Individuals with Disabilities Education Improvement Act (IDEA)?

A) Participating in selecting assessment instruments
B) Having education with students with similar disabilities
C) Participation in choosing service providers
D) Getting a free appropriate public education

CONTINUE ▶

**33**

Anton is a middle-school student with autism spectrum disorder (ASD). Which of the following would support him to be successful in his new placement?

A) Providing him with a visual schedule of daily activities
B) Allowing him to attend school for a half-day for the first month
C) Taking him on a tour of the school so that she can become familiar with the layout of the classrooms
D) Providing him with time away from her classmates when she has an outburst

**34**

Which of the following statements given below is a guaranteed right of due process for parents/guardians of children with disabilities?

A) Determining which assessments will be administered by each member of a school's multidisciplinary evaluation team
B) Providing a specific sequence of goals for their child's teachers and other service providers to address within a given school year
C) Viewing their child's comprehensive educational records at any point during the school year
D) Selecting a special education teacher within their school district to be their child's main teacher

**35**

How would a teacher attend to a kindergarten student with autism spectrum disorder who shows frustration due to limited speech and has a tendency to exhibit inappropriate behavior?

A) Refer the student to the office for disciplinary action if the student refuses to speak
B) Provide the student a way to communicate using augmentative communication
C) Avoid putting the student in situations where speech is required
D) Assist the student by completing what the student is perceived to be saying

**36**

Which of the following strategies would best address the goal of a special education teacher to promote the students' food preparation skills?

A) Asking students to choose a meal they would like to prepare and to work with them to write out the steps involved in making each food.

B) Providing direct instruction to students by planning opportunities for them to prepare various foods in school on a consistent basis.

C) Arranging for students to observe cafeteria staff while they are preparing food for lunch and meeting with the students to discuss their observations.

D) Sending a note to students parents/guardians requesting that students become involved in food preparation activities at home.

**37**

**The specific learning disability (SLD) is a** disorder in one or more of the basic psychological processes involved in understanding or in using language, spoken or written.

One of the students has a specific learning disability in Math class. For his individualized education program (IEP), which of the following should be included?

A) Reading problems to him during tests

B) Permitting him to use a calculator to solve word problems

C) Allowing him to answer word problems verbally during tests

D) Allowing him to use manipulatives to solve word problems

**38**

A special education teacher who co-teaches a culturally diverse second-grade class with several disabled students notices two students having difficulty paying attention to extended listening tasks such as teacher read-aloud. The teacher wonders if they have undiagnosed attention disorders.

Which of the following should the teacher first consider when reflecting on the situation?

A) It's possible that the students have not yet developed necessary expressive vocabulary skills that make them benefit from teacher read-aloud.
B) It's possible that the teacher may be unconsciously communicating lower expectations to these students.
C) It's possible that learning disabilities manifest themselves differently in students from different cultures.
D) It's possible that teacher-led activities may not be compatible with the personal and culturally influenced learning preferences of these students.

**39**

Which of the following is the skill acquired in vocabulary strategy instruction as an effective way of increasing students' reading comprehension?

A) Learn meanings of key terms in depth
B) Memorize lists of frequently used words
C) Focus on the importance of cognates
D) Identify synonyms and antonyms

**40**

Which of the following statements about IEP is correct regarding Individuals with Disabilities Education Act (IDEA)?

A) The IEP must not be made available to any school personnel except special education teachers.
B) The IEP must include a section on assistive devices, regardless of the nature or degree of the student's disability.
C) The IEP must be in effect before special education services or related services are provided.
D) The IEP must include a multiyear outline of instructional objectives.

**41**

Individualized Family Service Plan (IFSP) and Individualized Education Program (IEP) have a lot in common but how is IFSP differentiated from IEP?

A) It includes information on family support services, nutrition services, and case management.
B) It includes projected dates for the beginning of each service, and where each service will take place.
C) It includes a statement of the rights of parents or guardians to accept or decline any special education service.
D) It includes a statement of the child's strengths and needs.

**42**

Which would likely be the most difficult aspect of adulthood for a student with mild autism spectrum disorder and has received special education and speech-language services?

A) Establishing and maintaining quality interpersonal relationships
B) Obtaining a job within a field of interest
C) Living in an apartment or house independently
D) Managing personal finances

**43**

A science teacher for special education has observed that one of his students with the specific learning disability (SLD) is indeed active in class and punctual on homework; however, his reading comprehension score is low.

If there is an upcoming chapter test on next class, which of the following would be the most effective approach for his individualized education program (IEP)?

A) Reading the text aloud to him
B) Providing her frequent breaks during testing
C) Allowing the use of a dictionary to check spelling
D) Administering the test to her in a separate room

**44**

A year ago, Sally was diagnosed as emotionally disturbed. Then recently, she is becoming unresponsive to therapeutic interventions, and her cognitive abilities are lower than average.

What co-occurring condition can be diagnosed?

A) Mental Retardation
B) Autism
C) Specific Learning Disability
D) ADD

**45**

Which of the following would the individualized education program (IEP) team be responsible for when they recommend modifications to the student's transportation services and mobility supports during a meeting when some parents of disabled students are unable to attend?

A) Make plans to implement the modification and merely note the parent's absence at the meeting in the student's IEP file.

B) Notify student's transportation services and mobility provider about the upcoming changes.

C) Have a reevaluation of the need for a student for other instructional supports and related services in light of the modification.

D) Send a document of the IEP modifications and the specific reasons for the recommendation to the parents.

**46**

Which of the following protection does section 504 of the Rehabilitation Act of 1973, a civil rights law against discrimination, provide students who attend a school that receives federal funds?

A) Discrimination based solely on an individual's socioeconomic status

B) Discrimination based solely on an individual's citizenship status

C) Discrimination based solely on an individual's gender or sexual orientation

D) Discrimination based solely on an individual's disability

**47**

**Asperger syndrome (AS)** is a developmental disorder characterized by significant difficulties in social interaction and nonverbal communication as well as restricted and repetitive patterns of behavior and interests.

With which of the following aspects of oral language development do elementary school students with Asperger syndrome typically have difficulty?

A) The use of appropriate intonation and inflection

B) The formation of complex spoken sentences

C) The expansion of their expressive vocabulary

D) The application of different verb tenses

**48**

Which of the following strategies would help a 4th-grade student with a specific learning disability that functions at a 2nd-grade level in the written expression for his upcoming curriculum-based social studies test involving writing an essay?

A) Individualizing the student's test to address content appropriate for the early elementary level

B) Giving the student an unlimited amount of time to complete the essay portion of the test

C) Allowing the student to complete the test using oral responses

D) Setting up a study carrel for the student to use when taking the test

**49**

What is the most appropriate role for the special education teacher in a full inclusion setting?

A) Planning of instruction with the general education teacher and co-teach all students in the class

B) Serving as an instructional assistant to the general education teacher

C) Observing the general education teacher at least once a week to discuss teaching strategies that seem to work well

D) Managing the behavior of the students receiving the special education while the general education teacher presents academic content

There is a disagreement of Darin's parents regarding the pull-out services three times a week in the resource room as he has a specific learning disability in reading comprehension.

According to federal law, which of the following best describes the next step in the situation?

A) Darin begins to receive the IEP teams recommended services until an agreement is reached.
B) Darin's parents initiate the due process and take the issue to meditation.
C) Darin is reevaluated independently by a community-based psychologist who reports the results to the team.
D) Darin's parents and their attorney take the issue to a fair hearing.

A student with an emotional/behavioral disability has persistent and consistent emotional or behavioral responses that adversely affect performance in the educational environment that cannot be attributed to age, culture, gender, or ethnicity.

Which of the following characteristics is included in the definition of an emotional or behavioral disability given above?

A) Significantly subaverage intellectual functioning
B) Inability to achieve satisfactory interpersonal relationships
C) Stereotyped and repetitive use of language
D) Inflexible adherence to specific, nonfunctional routines

**An ecological perspective** is an approach to social work practice that addresses the complex transactions between people and their environment.

In which of the following is the ecological perspective on emotional and behavioral disorders best described?

A) Inclusion settings are less beneficial for students with emotional and behavioral disorders than for students with other types of disabilities.

B) Poisons in the physical environment cause emotional and behavioral disorders.

C) Emotional and behavioral disorders involve interactions between the child and the child's social environment.

D) Children with emotional and behavioral disorders need exposure to an ever-broadening social environment.

## SECTION 2

| # | Answer | Topic | Subtopic | # | Answer | Topic | Subtopic | # | Answer | Topic | Subtopic | # | Answer | Topic | Subtopic |
|---|---|---|---|---|---|---|---|---|---|---|---|---|---|---|---|
| 1 | D | TA | SA1 | 14 | A | TA | SA2 | 27 | D | TA | SA2 | 40 | C | TA | SA2 |
| 2 | D | TB | SB2 | 15 | B | TB | SB2 | 28 | D | TA | SA1 | 41 | A | TA | SA2 |
| 3 | B | TA | SA2 | 16 | A | TA | SA2 | 29 | C | TB | SB2 | 42 | A | TB | SB1 |
| 4 | D | TB | SB2 | 17 | C | TA | SA1 | 30 | C | TA | SA1 | 43 | A | TA | SA2 |
| 5 | C | TA | SA2 | 18 | D | TB | SB2 | 31 | B | TB | SB1 | 44 | A | TA | SA1 |
| 6 | C | TA | SA1 | 19 | A | TB | SB2 | 32 | D | TA | SA2 | 45 | D | TA | SA2 |
| 7 | B | TA | SA2 | 20 | B | TA | SA1 | 33 | A | TB | SB2 | 46 | D | TB | SB2 |
| 8 | A | TB | SB1 | 21 | B | TB | SB2 | 34 | C | TA | SA1 | 47 | A | TA | SA1 |
| 9 | C | TA | SA1 | 22 | C | TB | SB2 | 35 | B | TB | SB1 | 48 | C | TB | SB2 |
| 10 | D | TB | SB2 | 23 | A | TB | SB1 | 36 | B | TB | SB2 | 49 | A | TB | SB1 |
| 11 | D | TB | SB2 | 24 | C | TA | SA1 | 37 | D | TA | SA2 | 50 | B | TB | SB1 |
| 12 | B | TA | SA2 | 25 | C | TB | SB1 | 38 | D | TB | SB1 | 51 | B | TA | SA1 |
| 13 | A | TB | SB2 | 26 | C | TA | SA1 | 39 | A | TB | SB2 | 52 | C | TB | SB2 |

## Topics & Subtopics

| Code | Description | Code | Description |
|---|---|---|---|
| SA1 | Understanding Disabilities | SB2 | Instructional Strategies |
| SA2 | Individualized Education Plan (IEP) | TA | Disabilities |
| SB1 | Collaboration & Communication | TB | Learning Environment |

# TEST DIRECTION

**DIRECTIONS**

Read the questions carefully and then choose the ONE best answer to each question.

Be sure to allocate your time carefully so you are able to complete the entire test within the testing session. You may go back and review your answers at any time.

You may use any available space in your test booklet for scratch work.

Questions in this booklet are not actual test questions but they are the samples for commonly asked questions.

This test aims to cover all topics which may appear on the actual test. However some topics may not be covered.

Studying this booklet will be preparing you for the actual test. It will not guarantee improving your test score but it will help you pass your exam on the first attempt.

**Some useful tips for answering multiple choice questions;**

- Start with the questions that you can easily answer.

- Underline the keywords in the question.

- Be sure to read all the choices given.

- Watch for keywords such as NOT, always, only, all, never, completely.

- Do not forget to answer every question.

**1**

Jane is a high school student with an intellectual disability.

Which of the following daily skills would be necessary to aid Jane?

A) Identifying the states on a map
B) Stating the main idea of a paragraph
C) Knowing the multiplication table
D) Using a microwave oven

**2**

Many children with emotional and behavioral disorders act impulsively and often exhibit anxiety.

Which of the following disorder is commonly associated with emotional and behavioral disorders?

A) Obsessive-compulsive disorder
B) A speech and language processing disorder
C) Attention-deficit/hyperactivity disorder (ADHD)
D) Autism spectrum disorder (ASD)

**3**

**Cystic fibrosis** is a progressive, genetic disease. It is a lifelong condition in which the glands that produce mucus, sweat, and intestinal secretions do not function properly.

Which of the following does a student with cystic fibrosis is most prone to?

A) Kidney failure
B) Migraine headaches
C) Brittle bones
D) Respiratory infection

**4**

Which of the following strategies would help an ESE (Exceptional Student Education) teacher who wants to help elementary students with intellectual disabilities develop and extend basic self-care skills such as grooming and personal hygiene?

A) Supplying art materials for students to use to depict individuals performing self-care activities
B) Providing direct instruction in the skills in natural contexts and environments
C) Supplying toothbrushes and other relevant tools for students to play with and explore creatively
D) Providing large cloth dolls for students to use to practice the skills

**5**

A student with specific learning disability receives a homework that needs word processing and speech recognition software. Which of the following would aid him to use assistive technology successfully?

A) Assigning keyboarding homework
B) Limiting the amount of written homework
C) Allowing choice of topic for written assignments
D) Providing software for home use

**6**

In a response to intervention (RTI) model, which of the following is a key component of all tiers of response?

A) Curriculum-based measurement
B) Small-group instruction
C) Shortened classroom assignments
D) One-on-one tutoring

**7**

What nondegenerative disorder affects motor function resulting from brain injury acquired before, during, or shortly after birth?

A) Muscular Dystrophy
B) Cerebral Palsy
C) Cystic Fibrosis
D) Multiple Sclerosis

**8**

Frequency recording is a simple counting of how many times a behavior occurs during a designated period of time.

Which of the following would illustrate data collection through frequency recoding?

A) Lisa screamed for 2 minutes.
B) Mandy bit her hand three times per minute.
C) It took 4 minutes for Sam to line up after the fire alarm went off during the drill.
D) When Romeo was given a mathematics problem, he kicked Alice and was sent to the office.

CONTINUE ▶

**9**

According to the IFSP guidelines, how many years old must a student be to be qualified for the program?

A) 1-3
B) 0-4
C) 0-7
D) 0-3

**10**

Summative assessments have a high point value. Which of the following is an example of a summative assessment?

A) Writing sentences using spelling words
B) An end of chapter test
C) Completing a cloze activity
D) Completing a homework assignment

**11**

Which of the following services could best help a student with cerebral palsy to walk in a balanced manner?

A) Occupational Therapist
B) Physical Therapist
C) Physical Education Teacher
D) Yoga Instructor

**12**

Which of the following learning strategies would most likely benefit a student with a tendency to speak a lot during the activities and move around the classroom?

A) Creating a picture book
B) Writing a poem
C) Acting out a scene from a play
D) Using manipulative in math

**13**

Which of the following services could best help a student who needs to develop fine motor skills?

A) Yoga instructor
B) Physical Education teacher
C) Occupational Therapist
D) Physical Therapist

**14**

Which of the following assessments would use student's classwork to evaluate progress and adapt instruction?

A) Summative assessment
B) Curriculum-based assessment
C) Guided practice
D) Standardized achievement testing

**15**

Which of the following is closely linked to the development of learned helplessness in students with learning disabilities?

A) Repeated academic failure
B) High parental expectations
C) Delayed physical growth
D) Mild cognitive deficit

**16**

Which of the following techniques is likely to be most successful for the learners with intellectual disabilities to retain previously acquired skills?

A) Acknowledging appropriate behavior regularly
B) Allowing longer independent practice periods
C) Providing periodic review of lessons
D) Scheduling frequent peer tutoring sessions

**17**

Which of the following may be a natural consequence for Daniel, a 10th-grade student diagnosed as Emotionally Disturbed, who tends to distract and speak out often without permission?

A) The student misses the instruction and does not complete the assignment.
B) The student is sent to the principal frequently.
C) The student acts out more in the classroom.
D) The student becomes popular in the classroom.

**18**

Jane was put in a small reading group to help her improve her reading skills. However, she was still struggling with reading despite the intervention. Thus, her teachers decided to refer her for Special Education services.

Which of the following does this situation illustrate?

A) The Response to Intervention model
B) Using appropriate summative assessments
C) The Functional Behavioral Assessment
D) The IQ Achievement Discrepancy model

**19**

Seating arrangements are the main part of a teacher's plan for classroom management. A third-grade student with a mild intellectual disability has been assigned to a cooperative cluster seating arrangement?

Which of the following would the seating arrangement's benefit?

A) He will be in closer proximity to the teacher.
B) He will be able to participate more in class discussions.
C) He can sit near the window.
D) He can work with a partner if he has questions.

**20**

Samantha, a 13-year old student with emotional problems has significant behavioral struggles that limit her ability to access her education.

Which service should be best recommended for her?

A) Physical Therapy
B) Speech and language
C) Behavioral Analysis Interventions
D) Occupational Therapy

**21**

Which of the following behavioral strategies would best help Trish, a student diagnosed with autism spectrum disorder (ASD), who experiences difficulty maintaining eye contact and makes impulsive comments during lessons?

A) Seating Trish next to the window so she can look outside
B) Providing Trish a visual menu of appropriate behaviors
C) Giving Trish high-interest, low-reading-level assignments
D) Assigning Trish a peer buddy to help her keep on task

**22**

Which of the following should Adam do to his students who are currently failing, disrupting peers and cannot be handled with previous rewards and consequences?

A) Discuss placement options with the parent to move the student to a more restrictive environment.
B) Issue a 5-day suspension from the class.
C) Hold an IEP meeting with the parent and admin to discuss the behavior and create a new BSP plan to address the problem behavior.
D) Give the student a week's worth of lunch detentions.

**23**

Ms. Carol wants to use a strategy that could most benefit her 4-year old pupil with mild autism to develop reading skills.

Which of the following strategies should Ms. Carol use?

A) Encourage the pupil's parents to read a book to him/her
B) Letting the pupil use graphic organizers while reading
C) Listening to an audio recording to follow how to read certain texts
D) Letting the pupil imitate the sounds needed to read words

**24**

Which of the following questions would be the most important for an IEP team to ask when considering how to incorporate an electronic communication board to the IEP of an elementary school student with ASD?

A) What previous experience does the student have using assistive devices such as electronic communication boards?
B) Which of the student's annual goals will the device enable him to meet?
C) How will the purchase and maintenance of the device be funded?
D) Are school staff members who work with the student trained in the proper use of electronic communication boards?

**25**

What would a middle school teacher of students with intellectual disabilities most likely do to promote the transfer of word attack skills to newspaper reading?

A) Develop writing exercises using words from the curriculum
B) Select articles from the local newspaper for students to read
C) Prepare worksheet exercises based on single sentences from newspaper articles
D) Prepare teacher-made newspaper articles for the students to read

**26**

What disorder is the most commonly co-occurring type of disability and is associated with emotional and behavioral disorders?

A) Autism spectrum disorder (ASD)
B) Attention-deficit/hyperactivity disorder (ADHD)
C) Obsessive-Compulsive Disorder (OCD)
D) A speech and language processing disorder

**27**

Josephine, a 6th-grade student with autism, is enrolled in a resource program. She has been observed to have demonstrated an inability to interact appropriately with peers.

Which service could best help Josephine?

A) Teach Josephine an SEL curriculum
B) Engaging Josephine in more group activities
C) Placing Josephine in an afterschool program
D) Therapist assistance

**28**

If a special education teacher was using a system that had escalating consequences, what would be an appropriate consequence for the third instance a Samantha speak without raising her hand?

A) Referral to an administrator
B) Having a brief meeting with the student to ask them to reflect on their behavior
C) Warning the student
D) Redirection to the correct behavior

**29**

**Fragile X syndrome** is a genetic condition that causes a range of developmental problems including learning disabilities and cognitive impairment.

Which of the following disabilities would likely show a developmental profile of social and emotional development similar to that of a child with fragile X syndrome?

A) Absence Seizure Disorder
B) Autism Spectrum Disorder
C) Muscular Dystrophy
D) Cerebral Palsy

**30**

What strategy would be most useful in addressing the actions of Deng, a student with a mild intellectual disability, that involves hugging peers and adults every time he sees them?

A) Using a verbal cue (e.g.,"use your words") to remind Deng not to hug others and to ask other teachers to do the same.
B) Teaching Deng appropriate ways to greet others and having him practice these greetings throughout the school day.
C) Talking with Deng about his classmates' reactions to being hugged and encouraging classmates to tell him if he makes them feel uncomfortable.
D) Providing Deng with a list of appropriate verbal and physical greetings (e.g., handshake, say "hello") to refer to throughout the day.

**31**

What would be the most important action of a student with a physical disability and depression undergoing a graduation and the transition from high school to college?

A) Reconsider whether going to college is a realistic goal.
B) Develop friendships with peers who have similar disabilities.
C) Rely more on family members regarding important decisions.
D) Learn how to access counseling services as needed.

**32**

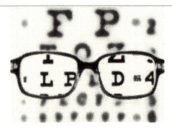

Which of the following is the best way for parents of Jan, a child with a visual impairment, to assess her recreational and leisure skills?

A) An evaluation by a trained specialist in visual disabilities
B) A conversation with a school counselor
C) A checklist from the expanded core curriculum
D) A classroom visit

**33**

It is not avoidable to have conflicts during unstructured playtime in kindergarten inclusion setting.

Which of the following would the teacher's main participation to solve the conflict?

A) To intervene and discipline children as soon as conflict occurs during an activity
B) To help children develop appropriate ways to resolve conflict
C) To reconsider the need for free play in the prekindergarten schedule
D) To teach children the essential features of good manners and etiquette

**34**

Which of the following types of assessment instruments must a special education teacher use in order to minimize bias when administering achievement assessments to elementary school students from culturally diverse backgrounds?

A) Screening
B) Authentic
C) Formative
D) Diagnostic

**35**

Why using research-based interventions regarding learning disabilities is most beneficial to the students?

A) Because the strategies and techniques used as interventions have been proven effective based on rigorous studies
B) Because school administrators and teachers think they are beneficial to students
C) Because parents support them
D) Because students find them enjoyable and easy to follow

**36**

People with disabilities are protected against discrimination in the workplace. Which legislation supports this provision?

A) Americans with Disabilities Act (ADA) of 1990
B) Individualized Education Program (IEP)
C) Section 504 of the Rehabilitation Act of 1973
D) Individuals with Disabilities Education Act (IDEA) of 2004

**37**

Motor skills are motions carried out when the brain, nervous system, and muscles work together.

For child ages 6 to 12 months, which of the following motor skills can be observed?

A) Sitting unassisted
B) Grasping objects
C) Rolling over
D) Walking downstairs

**38**

What is most likely included in the Individualized Family Service Plan (IFSP) for a 2-year-old child under the provisions of IDEA?

A) Techniques for the family to use in introducing academic subjects
B) Plans for making the transition into preschool
C) A recommendation of counseling for the child's siblings
D) A budget for early-intervention services

**39**

Which of the following is a chronic condition that affects millions of children and often continues into adulthood and includes a combination of persistent problems, such as difficulty sustaining attention, hyperactivity and impulsive behavior?

A) ADHD
B) Attention Deficit Disorder
C) ODD
D) All of above

**40**

Maria Montessori was an Italian physician and educator known for the educational philosophy bearing her name.

Which of the following special education approaches were most strongly influenced by her theories and philosophies?

A) A disabled child must begin vocational training as soon as possible.
B) Involvement of the family members in classroom work of the disabled child needing special education services should be done.
C) Education should be highly structured and ordered manner based on the child's chronological age.
D) Learning activities should be adjusted to each child's unique abilities, skills, and interests.

**41**

In measuring learning mastery, because of which of the following reasons a standardized achievement test is less preferred than a well-made teacher-developed test?

A) It allows comparison of students to each other
B) It has higher interrater reliability
C) It is more likely to yield a true score
D) It has better content validity

**42**

The cases of autism on a global scale are still rising. It is diagnosed across all age groups, though it is likely acquired upon birth.

Upon consulting the doctor, Simon's son was diagnosed with autism. How can the doctor best address this condition to Simon?

A) Explain his legal rights as a parent.
B) Explain to him that his son will have a different experience at school and life than other students, but an IEP will help her to reach goals that are specific to her abilities.
C) Let him know their life and family will never be the same again.
D) Let him feel compassion for his son's condition.

**43**

**Individualized Educational Plan (IEP)** is a program developed to ensure that a child who has a disability identified under the law and is attending an elementary or secondary educational institution receives specialized instruction and related services.

For students with IEPs, how should success be measured?

A) Amount of work a student has completed
B) Assessments based on SMART objectives
C) Class participation
D) State and District standardized Assessments

**44**

No Child Left Behind Act (NCLB) has which of the following effects upon special education practice?

A) Ensuring that each student receives a free and appropriate education.
B) Mandating that schools collaborate with community agencies when planning transition services.
C) Holding schools accountable for the learning of all students.
D) Providing funding for educational services for young children with disabilities.

**45**

Which step should a special education teacher take first regarding Lee, a student with cerebral palsy who uses communication board with speech output, to promote his communication skills within the new classroom environment?

A) Assigning the students in the general education class to write questions about Lee's communication board and having him answer the questions on his first day in class.

B) Asking the general education teacher to discuss with the class different ways in which people communicate, including using communication boards.

C) Having Lee introduce himself to the general education class and explain how and when he began using the communication board.

D) Ensuring that the general education teacher understands how Lee uses the communication board before his transition into the class.

**46**

**The Individuals with Disabilities Education Act (IDEA) is a four-part (parts A to D) piece of American legislation that ensures students with a disability are provided with free appropriate public education (FAPE) that is tailored for their individual needs.**

Which of the following instruments as stated in Part C of the IDEA is used to document and guide early intervention services for infants and toddlers with development delays?

A) Individualized Family Service Plan (IFSP)

B) Section 504 of the Rehabilitation Act of 1973

C) Individualized Transition Plan (ITP)

D) Individualized Education Program (IEP)

E) Individualized Education Program (IEP)

**47**

Vanessa, a 15-year old blind student is enrolled in general education classes. Despite her disability, she has able to perform at grade level.

Which assessment accommodation would benefit Vanessa farther?

A) Reading the test aloud and having Vanessa answer orally
B) Exempting Vanessa from taking tests
C) Giving shorter tests in Braille format
D) Giving tests and Vanessa's answers in Braille format

**48**

Which of the following strategies should a special educator co-teaching a first-grade class use in order for a student with pragmatic language disorder to benefit most from the speech-language therapy (SLT) services she is receiving?

A) Arranging for the SLT to support the student during circle time and cooperative group times.
B) Making a schedule for the SLT to work with the student during classroom discussions so that any statement he makes can be immediately clarified.
C) Having a chosen peer in the class work with the student and the SLT on a regular basis.
D) Reducing distractions due to the student and SLT working together by establishing a work area in the quiet area of the classroom.

**49**

Which of the following factors should help guide the student's individualized education program (IEP) team when determining the least restrictive environment (LRE) for a student with disabilities?

A) The collective opinion of the service providers who previously worked with the student.
B) The frequency, duration, and intensity of the identified services needed by the student.
C) The credentials and experience of the district professionals who work with the student when they are available.
D) The relative costs of the modifications, services, and placement options being considered for the student.

**50**

How does an Individualized Education Program (IEP) differ from an Individualized Family Service Plan (IFSP)?

A) IEP is primarily concerned with the student while IFSP is primarily concerned with the student's family.
B) IEP evaluates present levels of the student, while the IFSP evaluates the present levels the family members.
C) Only IEP has goals and objectives.
D) The services provided by IEP are directed to the student, while that of IFSP's are for the student's parents.

**51**

When the Individuals with Disabilities Act (IDEA) equips parents with the right to disagree with or deny an IEP and IEP team recommendations?

A) When the parents defend well the reasons for their disagreement
B) When a counter finding from a doctor or psychologist supports the parents' decision
C) When the parents do not yet have the said right
D) When the parents decide to disagree or deny the support regardless of proof or reasons

Rosie is already a 5th-grade student but has a 3rd-grade reading level. She's been given a special support due to her Specific Learning Disability. With this support, she was able to read grade-level phonics and developed word analysis skills in decoding single-syllabic words with 90% accuracy.

To further help Rosie improve her reading ability, which of the following annual goals is most appropriate to set for her?

A) Challenge her to improve her reading fluency rate.
B) Provide familiar reading materials so that she can self-correct word recognition.
C) Provide her with grade level texts to practice reading.
D) Read multisyllabic words so that she could apply her knowledge of all letter-sound correspondences, syllabication patterns, and morphology.

## SECTION 3

| # | Answer | Topic | Subtopic | # | Answer | Topic | Subtopic | # | Answer | Topic | Subtopic | # | Answer | Topic | Subtopic |
|---|---|---|---|---|---|---|---|---|---|---|---|---|---|---|---|
| 1 | D | TB | SB2 | 14 | B | TB | SB2 | 27 | A | TB | SB2 | 40 | D | TA | SA1 |
| 2 | C | TA | SA1 | 15 | A | TA | SA1 | 28 | B | TB | SB2 | 41 | D | TB | SB2 |
| 3 | D | TA | SA1 | 16 | C | TB | SB2 | 29 | B | TA | SA1 | 42 | B | TB | SB1 |
| 4 | B | TB | SB2 | 17 | A | TA | SA1 | 30 | B | TB | SB2 | 43 | B | TA | SA2 |
| 5 | D | TB | SB2 | 18 | A | TB | SB2 | 31 | D | TB | SB1 | 44 | C | TA | SA1 |
| 6 | A | TB | SB2 | 19 | D | TB | SB2 | 32 | C | TB | SB1 | 45 | D | TB | SB1 |
| 7 | B | TA | SA1 | 20 | C | TA | SA1 | 33 | B | TB | SB2 | 46 | A | TA | SA1 |
| 8 | B | TA | SA2 | 21 | B | TB | SB2 | 34 | B | TB | SB2 | 47 | A | TB | SB2 |
| 9 | D | TA | SA1 | 22 | C | TB | SB2 | 35 | A | TB | SB2 | 48 | A | TB | SB2 |
| 10 | B | TB | SB2 | 23 | C | TB | SB2 | 36 | A | TA | SA1 | 49 | B | TA | SA2 |
| 11 | B | TA | SA1 | 24 | B | TA | SA2 | 37 | A | TA | SA1 | 50 | A | TA | SA2 |
| 12 | C | TB | SB2 | 25 | B | TB | SB2 | 38 | B | TA | SA2 | 51 | D | TA | SA2 |
| 13 | C | TB | SB2 | 26 | B | TA | SA1 | 39 | D | TA | SA1 | 52 | D | TA | SA2 |

## Topics & Subtopics

| Code | Description | Code | Description |
|---|---|---|---|
| SA1 | Understanding Disabilities | SB2 | Instructional Strategies |
| SA2 | Individualized Education Plan (IEP) | TA | Disabilities |
| SB1 | Collaboration & Communication | TB | Learning Environment |

# TEST DIRECTION

**DIRECTIONS**

Read the questions carefully and then choose the ONE best answer to each question.

Be sure to allocate your time carefully so you are able to complete the entire test within the testing session. You may go back and review your answers at any time.

You may use any available space in your test booklet for scratch work.

Questions in this booklet are not actual test questions but they are the samples for commonly asked questions.

This test aims to cover all topics which may appear on the actual test. However some topics may not be covered.

Studying this booklet will be preparing you for the actual test. It will not guarantee improving your test score but it will help you pass your exam on the first attempt.

**Some useful tips for answering multiple choice questions;**

- Start with the questions that you can easily answer.

- Underline the keywords in the question.

- Be sure to read all the choices given.

- Watch for keywords such as NOT, always, only, all, never, completely.

- Do not forget to answer every question.

**1**

A direct reading instruction in decoding skills to facilitate word recognition of vocabulary words is given to Shane, a ninth-grade student with a specific learning disability (SLD).

Which approach or strategy is represented by this instruction?

A) A remedial approach
B) Scripted reading instruction
C) A metacognitive strategy
D) A compensatory approach

**2**

Which of the following symptoms would a fifth-grade student with Tourette syndrome show?

A) Paralyzed legs
B) Loss of visual ability
C) Hearing loss
D) Involuntary movements

**3**

Which of the following would be a teacher's first move to eliminate a behavior from a student's repertoire?

A) Make sure that the student agrees to the change.
B) Determine a more appropriate behavior to take its place.
C) Have an IEP meeting so that all team members agree.
D) Consult with a board-certified behavior analyst.

**4**

Which of the following will not positively impact Sally's learning who is a nine-year-old student with mild attention deficit disorder (ADD)?

A) Having a structured home environment where the parents continue to work with Sally
B) Being in a self-contained, special-ed classroom
C) Teaching to the student's learning modality preference
D) Having clear and structured transitions between assignments in class

**5**

Summative assessments are used to evaluate student learning, skill acquisition, and academic achievement.

Which of the following illustrates a summative assessment?

A) Completing a homework assignment
B) Practicing how to write the directions for baking a cake
C) An end of chapter test
D) Writing sentences using spelling words

**6**

A federal law called the Individuals with Disabilities Education Act (IDEA) requires that public schools create an IEP for every child receiving special education services.

Which of the following must IEP do to follow IDEA requirements?

A) The IEP must be in effect before special education services or related services are provided.
B) The IEP must not be made available to any school personnel except special education teachers.
C) The IEP must include a section on assistive devices, regardless of the nature or degree of the student's disability.
D) The IEP must include a multiyear outline of instructional objectives.

**7**

Which of the following might be the function of Fabian's behavior that makes him often wander the class, getting out of the seat without permission and distracting peers?

A) A sense of powerlessness
B) Unclear limits
C) Avoidance/Escape
D) Not enough information to determine

**8**

Which of the following gross-motor skills is usually developed last in human development?

A) Hopping
B) Catching a ball with two hands
C) Skipping
D) Climbing stairs

**9**

Which of the following parts of a functional curriculum is taking gender differences into account when a special education teacher is planning instruction significant?

A) Money management
B) Vocational skills
C) Leisure activities
D) Personal hygiene

**10**

Parents of a student who is an English language learner wants to use their first language rather than English to the scheduled three-year reevaluation meeting.

Which of the following would the special educator do to facilitate better communication in the conference?

A) Request that the school administrator hires a translator.
B) Learn to say some basic greetings in the parents' first language.
C) Provide a dictionary for the parents to use.
D) Ask the parents to bring a family member who speaks both languages.

**11**

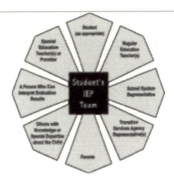

The Individualized Education Program (IEP) is a document that is developed for each public school child who needs special education.

Which of the following is an essential part of IEP?

A) Annual goals
B) Daily class schedule
C) Behavior intervention plan
D) Functional behavior assessment

**12**

Which of the following should be included in an IEP?

A) The present levels of academic achievement and functional performance
B) Suggestions for parental involvement
C) A description of the student's intellectual functioning
D) A record of past student performance

CONTINUE ▶

**13**

Which of the following ways could help a RTI team-best confirm that a student who is an English Language Learner (ELL) may have a mild intellectual disability?

A) By asking a colleague who is well versed in special education and ESL instruction to review the evaluation procedures for possible bias.
B) By using informal assessment procedures and instruments rather than formal standardized methods and tools to evaluate the student.
C) By recommending that the student is reevaluated using a different bilingual assessor and comparing the results of the two evaluations.
D) By meeting with the student's parents/guardians and an interpreter to inquire about the student's behaviors and abilities outside of school.

**14**

Considering differences in cultural and linguistical backgrounds, which factor is most important when assessing the academic achievement of students?

A) The students' prior opportunities to learn
B) The students' current grade level
C) The students' report card grades
D) The students' standardized district test scores

**15**

What step should an Individualized Education Program (IEP) team take first in supporting a successful transition for a ninth-grade student with specific learning disabilities and attention-deficit/hyperactivity disorder (ADHD)?

A) Identifying long-term post-secondary goals for the student's transition into community living.
B) Assessing the student's individual interests, preferences, and level of supports needed.
C) Determining how to measure the students progress toward transition goals.
D) Assessing the students need for assistive technology related to employment or post-secondary education.

**16**

**Trisomy 21** is a genetic order resulting from the presence of all or part of the third copy of chromosome 21.

Which of the following about trisomy 21 is not correct?

A) It is known as Down Syndrome
B) It is a chromosomal condition that affects development in females.
C) It often involves heart defects, visual and hearing impairments, and other health problems.
D) It involves birth defects, intellectual disabilities, characteristic facial features.

CONTINUE ▶

**17**

Samantha is a 2nd-grade student with Down syndrome having a low-average cognitive ability and poor social skills.

Which of the following strategies will help Samantha feel the most comfortable in her class?

A) Giving her consequences when she does not respond appropriately in a social situation
B) Structuring a daily 'buddy' interaction for her to partner with during play time
C) Creating more group activates that she can participate in
D) Spending the majority of her time by herself to avoid any social anxiety or pressure

**18**

Emotional disturbance in males has significantly higher rates than females.

Which of the following is the least likely reason for this discrepancy?

A) Females mature at an earlier age than males.
B) Males express their emotions physically while females do it verbally.
C) There is gender bias due to vagueness in ED qualifications.
D) Males have more cases of early trauma leading to violent outbursts.

**19**

**Full inclusion** means that all students, regardless of handicapping condition or severity, will be in a regular classroom full time.

Which is the most suited role for the special education teacher in full inclusion settings?

A) Serve as an instructional assistant to the general education teacher
B) Plan instruction with the general education teacher and co-teach all students in the class
C) Observe the general education teacher at least once a week in order to discuss teaching strategies that seem to work well
D) Manage the behavior of the students receiving the special education while the general education teacher presents academic content

**20**

After high school, which would be the most appropriate transition for Raul, a 12th-grade student who is on the autism spectrum, who has low cognitive abilities, low social skills, and is barely able to perform daily tasks?

A) Sending him to perform military duty
B) A trade school where he can learn a tactile craft
C) An adult ed program that continues to develop his independent living skills
D) Staying at home and helping around the house

**21**

An 8-year-old child with mild expressive language delay has normal hearing and age-appropriate functioning.

Which of the following placements would be best recommended?

A) A full-time general education placement with speech and language services
B) A full-time general education placement with an emphasis on reading support
C) A self-contained special education class with speech and language services
D) A part-time placement in a resource room for developmental and oral reading

**22**

An English language learner's academic achievement is significantly below grade level. Thus he is provided with an aide to translate assignments as well as tracking of the student's informal verbal interactions with classmates.

Which of the following information is most likely provided by these actions?

A) Whether the student's academic difficulties are related to language differences
B) Whether the student is motivated to achieve in the school
C) Whether the student's learning style is compatible with the teacher's instructional style
D) Whether the student is exhibiting a delay in social-emotional development

**23**

Which of the following techniques may be most helpful to Eric, who is an 11-year-old student with a mild Intellectual Disability, in studying ratios in his SDC class?

A) Using math manipulative.
B) Encouraging Eric with positive feedback and telling him he can do it.
C) Comparing and contrasting ratios.
D) Using concept development software.

**24**

What is the most important information for a special education teacher to know regarding an elementary school student with severe physical disabilities requiring adult assistance with feedings?

A) Whether the student is able to partially hold eating utensils or cups.
B) How much food and liquid the student commonly consumes at home.
C) Whether the student has demonstrated preferences for certain foods.
D) What type of consistency the student's foods and liquids should be.

### 25

**Task analysis** is the process of learning about ordinary users by observing them in action to understand in detail how they perform their tasks and achieve their intended goals.

Using task analysis in instructing students with disabilities, why is it the best fundamental rationale?

A) Instruction can be delivered effectively to many students at once without the need for individualization.

B) Students learn classification skills by identifying similar aspects of different kinds of tasks.

C) Instruction is delivered in steps that are easily achievable and that promote student success.

D) Students can eventually learn to analyze assigned tasks themselves.

### 26

Which strategy should a special education teacher implement first to prevent a student with posttraumatic stress disorder and symptoms of depression, from experiencing unnecessary anxiety?

A) Meeting with the student and reviewing the school's code of conduct.

B) Requesting that the student's parents meet with their child each morning to review his daily schedule.

C) Establishing a predictable routine for the student with advanced notice of changes.

D) Providing a quiet area in the school where the students can go to calm down.

**27**

For a child who is nonverbal, which of the following is an example of a functional language training?

A) Drilling on bilabial sounds so the child can say "mama"
B) Rewarding the child for any vocalization made while looking at the teacher
C) Rewarding the child for making a vocalization approximating a sound made by the teacher
D) Teaching the child to point to the sink when he or she wants a drink of water

**28**

Sandra, a second-grade student, has a low basic reading aptitude and been recommended for a comprehensive evaluation.

Which of the following should the multidisciplinary team members do prior to the assessment process?

A) Selecting appropriate instruments to administer to the student
B) Obtaining written permission from the student's parents or guardians
C) Reviewing the student's school and medical records
D) Observing the student in various school settings

**29**

Which of the following would best interpret Mark's score of 72% on the standardized achievement test?

A) Twenty-eight students within the test's norm group scored lower than Mark.
B) Mark answered 28 of 100 test items incorrectly.
C) Mark scored the same as or higher than 72 percent of the students in the test's norm group.
D) Mark answered 72 of the test items correctly.

**30**

What should a special education teacher do first if a student with epilepsy that involves generalized tonic-clonic seizures has a seizure?

A) Attempt to gently restrain the student to minimize muscle jerks.
B) Remove objects located around or near the student that could possibly cause injury.
C) Call or locate the school nurse to attend to the student.
D) Place an object such as a belt or wallet in the student's mouth to keep the airway open.

CONTINUE ▶

**31**

Which of the following deliberations must be emphasized by the Individual Family Service Plan (IFSP) team members in order to best ensure the selection of effective and appropriate services and supports for the plan stated in the IFSP of a 2-year-old child?

A) The methods that will be used to monitor and evaluate the child's progress
B) The current strengths and skills exhibited by the child in various domains
C) The resources available in local preschools the child may attend in the future
D) The educational background of the adults who will work with the child at home

**32**

Which of the following reflects the best practice in communicating the evaluation results to the parents of a 4-year-old child who was referred to a multidisciplinary team for an evaluation to determine if he meets the criteria for autism spectrum disorder (ASD)?

A) Describing the child's behavior using concrete observable examples across settings.
B) Using general statements to suggest the need to gather more behavioral information.
C) Using professional terms to support the behavioral diagnosis.
D) Comparing the child's behavior using normative samples.

**33**

In instructing students with disabilities, which of the following is the best rationale for using task analysis?

A) Instruction is delivered in steps that are easily achievable and that promote student success.
B) Instruction can be delivered effectively to many students at once without the need for individualization.
C) Students learn classification skills by identifying similar aspects of different kinds of tasks.
D) Students can eventually learn to analyze assigned tasks themselves.

**34**

Joey experiences a high anxiety when transitioning from class to lunch time. What strategy could best help this student?

A) Make a daily schedule for Joey to go in and out of the class before and after lunch
B) Allow Joey to leave the room earlier than his classmates to eat his lunch
C) Provide Joey a separate space where he can eat his lunch
D) Regularly remind Joey when it's almost time for lunch

**35**

The special education teacher is responsible for overseeing the work of the new paraeducators assigned to students with multiple disabilities.

Which of the following strategies would be best for monitoring the paraeducator's services provided to their assigned student?

A) Meeting with the paraeducator at the beginning and end of each week to conduct planning and debriefing sessions.

B) Asking the four paraeducators to spend some of their free time observing one another provide mutual advice and support.

C) Scheduling a weekly meeting with the four paraeducators to conduct a comprehensive discussion of their activities and concerns.

D) Enlisting the help of the general education teacher in planning and supervising the work of the new paraeducator.

**36**

In teaching problem-solving skills to students with learning disabilities, a special education teacher discovered a new instructional method.

Which resources would contain the most reliable research-based information on this new instructional method?

A) A mission statement posted by the Website of a company that publishes materials based on the new instructional method.

B) A peer-reviewed article about the new instructional method published in a special education journal.

C) Testimonial by teachers at a state-wide conference who have used the new instructional method in their classroom.

D) Postings about the new instructional method on a listserv for special education teachers.

**37**

For the benefit of which of the following is Assistive Technology used in the classrooms?

A) Physically handicapped students
B) Deaf or hard of hearing students
C) Visually impaired students
D) Any student who needs extra support in order to reach their educational needs as indicated in an IEP

**38**

Which data below is most accurate to use when presenting an IEP progress?

A) Informal observations made by the teacher
B) Self and peer evaluations of the student's work
C) Evidence of work collected regularly on a weekly basis
D) Assignment completion rate

**39**

A 9th-grade student always forgets to turn his assignments within the set deadline. Often time, he submits partial outputs only, and hence he receives failing grades.

Which skill should be developed to help the student overcome this weakness?

A) Self-regulation strategies
B) Note-taking skills
C) Mnemonic strategies
D) Time management skills

**40**

A first-grade student with fine-motor deficits will receive instruction in the general education classroom with supplementary aids and services as determined by an IEP team.

Which of the following provisions in the IEP would most likely best address the student's motor deficits?

A) Using more lenient or flexible criteria to grade the student on tasks involving fine-motor skills
B) Allowing the student to choose if he would participate in activities that require the use of fine-motor skills
C) Providing the student with multiple accommodations for physically performing tasks involving fine-motor skills
D) Providing the student with alternate activities when the class is doing work that requires fine-motor skills

CONTINUE ▶

**41**

Queenie, a 12th-grade student, has a cognitive ability level equivalent to average 13-year-old students. She struggles to complete tasks independently but has shown a strong interest in the cooking activities done in class.

Which of the following goals is most beneficial for Queenie?

A) Get a job in her preferred field after high school.
B) Attend a community college after high school.
C) Cook three simple meals for herself.
D) Live independently in an apartment.

**42**

Why do teachers need to conduct informal assessment?

A) Because it helps in determining whether the students have already mastered a certain concept or not.
B) Because it helps in determining how certain students perform in comparison to their classmates.
C) Because it helps in evaluating each student's learning progress.
D) Because it helps in evaluating whether or not students can pass the formative assessments.

**43**

Which of the following goals is not an important part of determining a student's annual Individualized Education Program (IEP)?

A) Identifying goals that are measurable and achievable
B) Aligning goals with common core standards
C) Evaluating the student's present achievement levels
D) Providing the same goals to all students to make teaching easier

**44**

The ecological perspective on emotional and behavioral disorders can be best defined by which of the following statements?

A) Inclusion settings are less beneficial for students with emotional and behavioral disorders than for students with other types of disabilities.
B) Emotional and behavioral disorders involve interactions between the child and the child's social environment.
C) Poisons in the physical environment cause emotional and behavioral disorders.
D) Children with emotional and behavioral disorders need exposure to an ever-broadening social environment.

**45**

Most of the students in an 8th-grade SDC class with diverse disabilities are performing 2-3 years below grade level.

Which assessment type for a summative world history test would be most appropriate to use for this class?

A) Multiple Choice
B) Open-ended questions
C) True or False
D) Matching-sequence

**46**

Samantha has demonstrated an ability to remain in class without disrupting the learning environment below her targeted goal. As an intervention, she is placed in an SDC setting for 60% of the school day and in general education for 40%.

Which of the following actions should the IEP team do after her annual review to help her reach her goal?

A) Remove her intervention services
B) Provide her a more restrictive environment
C) Provide her a less restricitve environment
D) Determine what other intervention may help her reach her goal based on re-evaluation results of her services

**47**

Despite being stated in her IEP that a student with autism spectrum disorder (ASD) should be included in the general education class she has been attending, the general education teacher has made little effort to do so. So, the special educations teacher helping the disabled student decided to spend more time in the classroom to help facilitate her integration into the class as well as speak to the general education teacher about including her in class.

Which of the following does the special education teacher's action show?

A) Her understanding of how to fulfill the role of consultant to school personnel who serve students with disabilities.
B) Her understanding of how to advocate for the needs and rights of students with disabilities.
C) Her understanding of how to reflect on personal biases as related to teaching students with disabilities.
D) Her understanding of how to engage in lifelong professional growth as related to teaching students with disabilities.

**48**

A fifth-grade teacher asks an IEP team of a fifth-grader with specific learning disability and ADHD to consider whether the student would benefit from receiving some of her services in an alternative setting because the student has not made expected academic or behavioral progress despite the teacher implementing all the modifications in the student's IEP.

Which of the following would be the best initial response the IEP team have in this situation?

A) The IEP should evaluate if the adjustments to the student's classroom instruction might lead to greater success.
B) The IEP should arrange for a paraeducator to be assigned to work with the student in her current placement.
C) The IEP should inform the student of the teacher's concerns and ask what she thinks of the proposed change.
D) The IEP should schedule daily study periods for the student in the resource room with the special education teacher.

## SECTION 4

| # | Answer | Topic | Subtopic | # | Answer | Topic | Subtopic | # | Answer | Topic | Subtopic | # | Answer | Topic | Subtopic |
|---|---|---|---|---|---|---|---|---|---|---|---|---|---|---|---|
| 1 | A | TB | SB2 | 13 | D | TA | SA2 | 25 | C | TB | SB2 | 37 | D | TA | SA2 |
| 2 | D | TA | SA1 | 14 | A | TB | SB2 | 26 | C | TB | SB1 | 38 | C | TA | SA2 |
| 3 | B | TB | SB2 | 15 | B | TA | SA2 | 27 | D | TB | SB2 | 39 | A | TB | SB2 |
| 4 | B | TB | SB2 | 16 | B | TA | SA1 | 28 | B | TB | SB2 | 40 | C | TA | SA2 |
| 5 | C | TB | SB2 | 17 | B | TB | SB2 | 29 | C | TB | SB2 | 41 | C | TA | SA1 |
| 6 | A | TA | SA2 | 18 | D | TA | SA1 | 30 | B | TA | SA1 | 42 | C | TB | SB2 |
| 7 | D | TA | SA1 | 19 | B | TB | SB2 | 31 | B | TA | SA2 | 43 | D | TA | SA2 |
| 8 | C | TA | SA1 | 20 | C | TB | SB2 | 32 | A | TB | SB1 | 44 | B | TA | SA1 |
| 9 | D | TB | SB2 | 21 | A | TB | SB2 | 33 | A | TB | SB2 | 45 | A | TB | SB2 |
| 10 | A | TB | SB1 | 22 | A | TB | SB2 | 34 | A | TA | SA1 | 46 | D | TA | SA2 |
| 11 | A | TA | SA2 | 23 | A | TB | SB2 | 35 | D | TB | SB2 | 47 | B | TA | SA2 |
| 12 | A | TA | SA2 | 24 | D | TA | SA1 | 36 | B | TB | SB2 | 48 | A | TA | SA2 |

## Topics & Subtopics

| Code | Description |
|---|---|
| SA1 | Understanding Disabilities |
| SA2 | Individualized Education Plan (IEP) |
| SB1 | Collaboration & Communication |
| SB2 | Instructional Strategies |
| TA | Disabilities |
| TB | Learning Environment |

# TEST DIRECTION

**DIRECTIONS**

Read the questions carefully and then choose the ONE best answer to each question.

Be sure to allocate your time carefully so you are able to complete the entire test within the testing session. You may go back and review your answers at any time.

You may use any available space in your test booklet for scratch work.

Questions in this booklet are not actual test questions but they are the samples for commonly asked questions.

This test aims to cover all topics which may appear on the actual test. However some topics may not be covered.

Studying this booklet will be preparing you for the actual test. It will not guarantee improving your test score but it will help you pass your exam on the first attempt.

**Some useful tips for answering multiple choice questions;**

- Start with the questions that you can easily answer.

- Underline the keywords in the question.

- Be sure to read all the choices given.

- Watch for keywords such as NOT, always, only, all, never, completely.

- Do not forget to answer every question.

**1**

For a high school student with an intellectual disability, which of the following would be an essential daily-living skill?

A) Identifying the states on a map
B) Using a microwave oven
C) Stating the main idea of a paragraph
D) Knowing the multiplication table

**2**

Which of the following behavioral strategies would help a fifth-grade student with autism spectrum disorder (ASD) to minimize her difficulty in maintaining eye contact and making impulsive ideas during class?

A) Provide a visual menu of appropriate behaviors
B) Assign a peer buddy to help him keep on task
C) Give him high-interest, low-reading-level assignments
D) Seat him next to the window so she can look outside

**3**

Which of the following steps should be taken when a student like Raphael who has Down syndrome is repeatedly bullied and harassed by his peers?

A) Send Raphael to a different school, so he is no longer bullied.
B) Give the phone number of the bullies' parents to Raphael's parents so that they can intervene directly.
C) Create a response plan of what the consequences will be for the students if they continue to bully Raphael and discuss it with the students' parents.
D) Talk to Raphael to help him understand what he might be doing to get bullied and help him to change the behavior.

**4**

A mother of a high school student with an intellectual disability wants to introduce a useful everyday acquired skill to his son.

Which of the following would be most essential?

A) Using a microwave oven
B) Knowing the multiplication table
C) Stating the main idea of a paragraph
D) Identifying the states on a map

CONTINUE ▶

### 5

Which is the most appropriate mathematics classes for Jen, a 7th-grade student with a special learning disability, that has mathematics achievement score indicating a stanine of 9?

A) Standard mathematics
B) Functional mathematics
C) Remedial mathematics
D) Advanced mathematics

### 6

Which of the following is the best and realistic way of dealing with one's own personal biases?

A) Working only with people whom you have no biases against
B) Understanding one's own biases in order to limit their impact
C) Ignoring all personal biases
D) Unloading all your personal biases

### 7

Which of the following types of assessments should a special education teacher use to collect diagnostic information on a third-grade student's reading ability in areas of decoding, vocabulary, and fluency?

A) Curriculum-based measurement
B) Informal reading inventory
C) Benchmark for learning outcomes
D) Standardized reading achievement test

### 8

Which of the following is required to refer a student for a formal evaluation to determine whether special education services are appropriate?

A) Physician referral
B) Teacher referral
C) The verbal agreement provided by the parents
D) Signed parental permission

**9**

What do you call the process of using word processing device that Laura, who is diagnosed with a specific learning disability, may use in doing all of her written tasks?

A) Assistive Technology
B) Coping Skills
C) Self-management
D) Writing Modification

**10**

Community-Based Instruction (CBI) is an educational instruction in naturally occurring community environments providing students "real life experiences".

Which of the following depicts community-based instruction?

A) Paying for a game of bowling
B) Sorting a variety of coins at home
C) Counting money in the classroom
D) Purchasing lunch in the school cafeteria

**11**

**Fluency** is the ability to read a text accurately, quickly, and with expression.

Which of the following strategy for increasing fluency does a teacher perform when he reads a passage to his students and asks them to repeatedly read the passage as a group?

A) Timed reading
B) Choral reading
C) Sight reading
D) Independent reading

**12**

What kind of educational measurement does an ESE teacher show by systematically collecting previously completed assessments of students?

A) Alternative assessment
B) Summative assessment
C) Portfolio assessment
D) Cognitive assessment

**13**

A student with ADD struggles with higher order thinking skills but is able to classify relationships and events effectively.

Which of the following would be the most appropriate assessment type to use for this kind of student?

A) Oral, short answer exam
B) Multiple choice
C) Matching-sequence
D) Essay

**14**

Which of the following type of classroom setting does Joaquin attend if he is in a gen-ed setting for most of the day and receives small group instruction in reading once a day?

A) Separate Day School
B) Inclusion program
C) Resource pull out services
D) Separate Day Class

**15**

Which formative assessment is most appropriate to use for a 5th grade deaf and hard of hearing class?

A) Oral recitation
B) Written exam tests
C) Answering questions through drawing
D) Asking students to signal thumbs up or thumbs down in response to a check for understanding

**16**

Which formative assessment can be a good source of data needed to write a behavioral intervention plan for students with severe behavioral problems?

A) The school disciplinary record
B) Classroom observations
C) The Woodcock-Johnson results
D) Standardized tests

**17**

Which of the following must be included in an Individualized Family Service Plan (IFSP)?

A) A comprehensive list of community organizations, service agencies, and support groups available to meet the family's needs

B) A report explaining the results of a formal psychological assessment of the family's functioning

C) A statement describing the family's concerns, priorities, strengths, and needs as these relate to their child's development

D) A projected list of dates for routine weekly family-teacher conferences to monitor the child's progress

**18**

Which of the following could be the most probable reason why a well-made teacher-developed test is most preferred to a standardized achievement test in measuring learning?

A) Better content validity
B) Allows comparison of students to each other
C) More likely to yield a true score
D) Higher interrater reliability

**19**

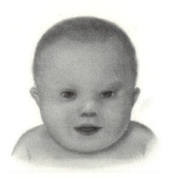

Down syndrome can be acquired from which of the following factors?

A) Chromosomal abnormality
B) Prenatal exposure to high amounts of alcohol
C) Oxygen deprivation during the birthing process
D) Neural tube defects

**20**

Autism is associated with low cognitive skills. Patients with this condition learn through a system of consequences and rewards for specific behaviors.

What can be done to aid their learning?

A) Use cognitivism approach
B) Use ecological approach
C) Use kinesthetic preference
D) Use behaviorism approach

**21**

What type of grouping strategy should Mr. Noto use to best support his 7th-grade SDC students diagnosed with ED who are struggling in building relationships and have a significant behavioral issue?

A) Mixed level base groups
B) Formal homogenous groups
C) Only independent work
D) Informal pairing

**22**

Gem, a 17-year-old student with a learning disability in mathematics, wants to be more actively involved in personal educational planning as she neglected it in previous years.

Which of the following should be her teacher best response?

A) Discussing the IEP with the student and assisting in identifying topics the student would like to address at the next IEP meeting
B) Suggesting that the student write a letter to the IEP team offering reasons for wanting to participate in IEP decision making
C) Providing the student with copies of laws and other materials related to IEP development and implementation
D) Asking the student to read the current IEP and suggest some specific goals for next year's IEP

**23**

Which component must be included in the students' Individualized Education Program (IEP), after an IEP team has acknowledged their eligibility for special education services?

A) A detailed plan for fully supporting the students' upcoming transition

B) A description of how the team plans to monitor the students' progress

C) A statement naming a designated service coordinator to implement the program

D) A statement reflecting the family's desired academic outcome for the students

**24**

What should be the first step in conducting Functional Behavioral Assessment (FBA) for a student with learning disability and attention-deficit/hyperactivity disorder (ADHD)?

A) Observe the students behavior across school settings.

B) Identify effective behavior self-monitoring strategies.

C) Define the student's behavior in measurable terms.

D) Develop a positive behavior support plan.

**25**

Ms. Monroe will be creating a unit plan. What should she first determine in writing the unit plan?

A) The type of diagnostic assessment to use

B) The types of formative assessments to use

C) The summative assessments to use

D) The learning competencies that students should master

**26**

The Individualized Educational Plan (IEP) is a plan or program developed to ensure that a child who has a disability identified under the law and is attending an elementary or secondary educational institution receives specialized instruction and related services.

Which of the following is necessary for an IEP?

A) A record of past student performance

B) Suggestions for parental involvement

C) A description of the student's intellectual functioning

D) The present levels of academic achievement and functional performance

CONTINUE ▶

**27**

What would be your first steps in planning if you were teaching a mixed 9th - 12th grade Special Day Class in English?

A) Research IEP goals and create learning profiles
B) Write curriculum that meets the individualized needs of students
C) Assign students to groups for flexible grouping
D) Create individualized goals for students

**28**

What strategy should a teacher use to improve a students' self-management skills to prevent tapping, humming, and stomping during quiet work times?

A) Creating a behavior chart totally how often the student engages in distracting behaviors and providing a reward as he reduces these behaviors.
B) Developing a visual cue to use with the student to help increase his awareness of when he is engaging in distracting behaviors.
C) Having the student move his desk to work in a separate area of the classroom when he becomes distracting to others.
D) Meeting with the student each morning to review the behaviors he needs to reduce and providing him with feedback about his progress at the end of each day.

**29**

Which strategy would most benefit the 8th-grade students with disabilities in learning multi-step linear equations?

A) Using supplemental curriculum to clarify learning misconceptions
B) Using a functional curriculum in exploring learning activities
C) Using of task scaffolding to assist students in step-by-step learning
D) Using of material scaffolding to practice various types of multi-step problems

**30**

A fifth-grade student with ADHD and specific learning disabilities who receives special education services is found to be easily distracted. He fidgets with school materials when he is seated at his desk and tends to disturb his classmates.

Which of the following aspects should be altered for a special education teacher to effectively accommodate this student's learning and behavioral needs during classroom assessments?

A) Presentation
B) Response
C) Setting
D) Schedule

**31**

Visual motor deficit affects the understanding of information that a person sees, or the ability to draw or copy.

Which of the following would an ESE teacher recommend to a 2nd-grade teacher about a student's having visual motor deficits?

A) Refer the student to the occupational therapist for an evaluation.
B) Request an initial evaluation of the student's academic aptitude.
C) Document the student's response to general education intervention strategies.
D) Develop individualized programming to meet the student's needs.

**32**

Individuals with autism spectrum disorder (ASD) and individuals with nonverbal learning disabilities often experience difficulties with communication.

Which of the following would be their similarities?

A) Good organizational skills
B) Preference for visual-spatial tasks
C) Difficulty interpreting social cues
D) Limited range of interests

**33**

Liza is a middle-school student with autism spectrum disorder (ASD).

Which of the following supports is most likely to help Liza be successful in her new placement?

A) Taking Liza on a tour of the school so that she can become familiar with the layout of the classrooms
B) Providing Liza with a visual schedule of daily activities
C) Providing Liza with time away from her classmates when she has an outburst
D) Allowing Liza to attend school for a half - day for the first month

**34**

Which of the following assessments is an example of a formative assessment in the topic about the theory of evolution, with an 8th-grade SDC class?

A) Submitting an exit ticket at the end of each lesson
B) Answering a pre-test to assess the students' prior knowledge about the topic
C) Answering a unit exam after finishing the unit
D) Submitting a research project about the evolution of certain animal species

CONTINUE ▶

**35**

Two teachers, one a general education and the other a special education teacher, are co-teaching an ELA class, whose small group of students struggle with basic literacy skills.

Which co-teaching model would be most appropriate to use to help the struggling students?

A) Parallel teaching
B) Station teaching
C) Lesson Study
D) Alternative teaching

**36**

For a 10th grade class for students who are diagnosed as emotionally disturbed, which of the following behavior management models would be most appropriate?

A) Gordon's teacher effectiveness training
B) Canter's Assertive Discipline model
C) Any non-interventionist model
D) Glasser's Reality model

**37**

A student is enrolled in a resource program. Who is responsible for monitoring the student's academic progress?

A) The general education teacher
B) The resource teacher
C) Both the general education teacher and the resource teacher
D) The school principal

**38**

During a meeting with the parents of a third-grade student with an IEP who requires an interpreter, a special education teacher makes a point of addressing his questions and responses to the interpreters and uses the time the interpreter is listening to the parents' responses and comments to take down notes.

Which of the following is the most significant problem with the teacher's approach?

A) He assumes the parents would be comfortable using an interpreter they don't know.
B) He shows lack of respect for the parents by speaking to them through the interpreter and not them directly.
C) He keeps a written record of the parents' comments and concerns.
D) He neglects to ask the student to translate for her parents instead of the interpreter.

**39**

Which of the following styles will encourage learning for students with attention deficit disorder (ADD)?

A) Use sounds and music
B) Use lectures and writings
C) Use body movements and sense of touch
D) Use picture and image

**40**

A certain school requires sending home progress reports every 6 weeks.

How often should a teacher in this school update the parents of the students' performances?

A) Every week
B) Twice a week
C) Every 6 weeks
D) Every annual IEPs session

**41**

Which of the following is the primary purpose of administering a universal screening to all kindergarten students three times during the school year?

A) To establish a baseline that would be used to monitor individual student progress
B) To gather student data so that first-grade teachers can effectively develop curriculum content
C) To identify those students who may be at risk and in need of additional behavioral and instructional support
D) To determine why students are underperforming and in need of individualized special education instruction

**42**

Raymond is an autistic 9th-grade student who performs at a 4th grade level in reading, writing, and math.

If you were her teacher, which type(s) of assessment should you recommend for him?

A) Formal Assessments
B) Summative Assessments
C) Informal Assessments
D) All of the above

### 43

Jenny, a student with Down Syndrome with an average social ability and slightly below average cognitive ability, has been enrolled in an inclusion classroom.

Which transitional daily living goal is most appropriate for Jenny's case?

A) Immersing in community projects
B) Enrolling in a community college
C) Cooking daily meals for herself and others
D) Assisted living program

### 44

Several students in a third-grade class had reading scores below the district benchmark. Which action should the classroom teacher take first based on the response to intervention (RTI) procedures?

A) Continue to collect data on each student's reading performance using curriculum-based measures.
B) Develop a student intervention plan for differentiating small-group reading instruction for these students.
C) Refer each of the students for a comprehensive, individualized evaluation.
D) Request that the special education teacher provide these students with reading instruction in the third-grade classroom.

### 45

Which of the following factors would be most important for an IEP team developing an annual IEP for a 5-year-old student with significant developmental delays to take into account when creating goals for fostering the students' self-help skills?

A) The types of self-help skills a typical 5-year-old would be able to perform.
B) The availability of adaptive equipment for performing self-help skills.
C) The level of interest the student has in learning self-help skills.
D) The family's attitudes and understanding about the development of self-help skills.

### 46

It is important to do progress monitoring consistently over the course of the school year primarily because

A) It helps to determine what changes in assessment format are necessary to do
B) It informs necessary adjustments to be made in lesson planning
C) It helps determine if adjustments are needed for student goals
D) It is an administrative requirement

**47**

Down syndrome, also known as trisomy 21, is a genetic disorder that is caused by the presence of all or part of the third copy of chromosome 21. It is typically associated with growth delays and average IQ.

Which of the following health problems would a child with Down syndrome have a higher risk of developing as compared to typical children?

A) Heart defects
B) Brain aneurysms
C) Spastic muscles
D) Hardening of the arteries

**48**

The Individuals with Disabilities Education Act (IDEA) emphasized that students with special needs should be put in the least restrictive environment as much as possible.

What does it imply to educators?

A) Students with disabilities should be provided with the restrictions that other students have on their education.
B) Students with disabilities should be given the least amount of choices in where to go to school.
C) Students with disabilities should be with their general education peers as much as possible.
D) Students with disabilities should be placed in a smaller environment away from distractions.

# SECTION 5

| # | Answer | Topic | Subtopic |
|---|--------|-------|----------|
| 1 | B | TA | SA1 |
| 2 | A | TB | SB2 |
| 3 | C | TB | SB2 |
| 4 | A | TB | SB2 |
| 5 | D | TB | SB2 |
| 6 | B | TB | SB2 |
| 7 | B | TB | SB2 |
| 8 | D | TB | SB2 |
| 9 | A | TB | SB2 |
| 10 | A | TB | SB2 |
| 11 | B | TB | SB2 |
| 12 | C | TB | SB2 |
| 13 | C | TB | SB2 |
| 14 | C | TB | SB2 |
| 15 | D | TB | SB2 |
| 16 | B | TB | SB2 |
| 17 | C | TA | SA2 |
| 18 | A | TB | SB2 |
| 19 | A | TA | SA1 |
| 20 | D | TB | SB2 |
| 21 | A | TB | SB2 |
| 22 | A | TB | SB1 |
| 23 | B | TA | SA2 |
| 24 | C | TA | SA1 |
| 25 | C | TB | SB2 |
| 26 | D | TA | SA2 |
| 27 | A | TB | SB2 |
| 28 | B | TB | SB2 |
| 29 | C | TB | SB2 |
| 30 | C | TB | SB2 |
| 31 | C | TB | SB1 |
| 32 | C | TA | SA1 |
| 33 | B | TB | SB1 |
| 34 | A | TB | SB2 |
| 35 | D | TB | SB1 |
| 36 | B | TB | SB2 |
| 37 | C | TB | SB1 |
| 38 | B | TB | SB1 |
| 39 | C | TB | SB2 |
| 40 | C | TB | SB2 |
| 41 | C | TB | SB2 |
| 42 | D | TB | SB2 |
| 43 | C | TB | SB2 |
| 44 | A | TB | SB2 |
| 45 | D | TA | SA2 |
| 46 | B | TB | SB2 |
| 47 | A | TA | SA1 |
| 48 | C | TA | SA1 |

## Topics & Subtopics

| Code | Description |
|------|-------------|
| SA1 | Understanding Disabilities |
| SA2 | Individualized Education Plan (IEP) |
| SB1 | Collaboration & Communication |
| SB2 | Instructional Strategies |
| TA | Disabilities |
| TB | Learning Environment |

# TEST DIRECTION

**DIRECTIONS**

Read the questions carefully and then choose the ONE best answer to each question.

Be sure to allocate your time carefully so you are able to complete the entire test within the testing session. You may go back and review your answers at any time.

You may use any available space in your test booklet for scratch work.

Questions in this booklet are not actual test questions but they are the samples for commonly asked questions.

This test aims to cover all topics which may appear on the actual test. However some topics may not be covered.

Studying this booklet will be preparing you for the actual test. It will not guarantee improving your test score but it will help you pass your exam on the first attempt.

**Some useful tips for answering multiple choice questions;**

- Start with the questions that you can easily answer.

- Underline the keywords in the question.

- Be sure to read all the choices given.

- Watch for keywords such as NOT, always, only, all, never, completely.

- Do not forget to answer every question.

**1**

Which of the following is the usual problem involved in phonological difficulties at the receptive language level?

A) Articulating particular phonemes
B) Recognizing vowels
C) Producing consonants
D) Discriminating speech sounds

**2**

Differentiating instruction is a framework for effective teaching that provides different students with different avenues to learn in terms of acquiring content, making sense of ideas and developing teaching materials and assessment measures so that all students within a classroom can learn effectively, regardless of differences in ability.

Which of the following is an example of differentiating instruction?

A) Asking all the boys to make a poster and all the girls to write an essay
B) Allowing students to summarize a chapter with a poem, essay, or cartoon
C) Exempting half the class from a homework assignment
D) Assigning different students to read certain chapters of a read-aloud book

**3**

Which of the following is used in norm-referenced assessment to compare one student's performance on a test to the performance of other students' at her age if the assessment estimates whether the student's scores are above average, average, or below average compared to her peers?

A) Scaled score
B) Raw score
C) Standard score
D) Developmental score

**4**

Which of the following information about a student is provided by curriculum-based assessments?

A) Eligibility for special education services
B) Progress in acquiring specific academic skills
C) Aptitude for future academic success
D) Ability to use assistive technology to perform academically

**5**

Which of the following steps best help Wendy, a 7th-grade student with Down syndrome, improve in her math class?

A) Pairing her with another student who performs at the same level
B) Having her work independently
C) Grouping her with higher performing students
D) Placing her in an SDC math class

**6**

A second-grade teacher, the special education teacher, and the school nurse discussed the needs of the new student with a specific learning disability and severe asthma before the student's arrival.

Which best describes the second-grade teacher's primary role?

A) Develop the student's individualized instructional objectives.
B) Determine the student's grade equivalency.
C) Rank the student's abilities among peers.
D) Focus on the student's specific range of academic skills.

**7**

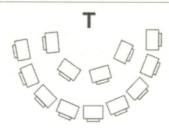

Which of the following would be the greatest effect of seating students in the semicircle?

A) Students can leave the classroom quickly.
B) The desks fit better in the classroom.
C) The teacher can easily monitor each student.
D) Students can easily work in small groups.

**8**

Summative assessment can be best illustrated by which of the following activities?

A) A test at the end of each chapter
B) Practicing how to write the directions for baking a cake
C) Completing a homework assignment
D) Writing sentences using spelling words

CONTINUE ▶

**9**

Fluency is the ability to read a text accurately, quickly, and with expression. When fluent readers read silently, they recognize words automatically. They group words quickly to help them gain meaning from what they read.

Which of the following belongs in improving reading fluency?

A) Reading and explaining passages longer than five sentences
B) Reading aloud with appropriate voice intonation and pauses
C) Reading choral responses with the entire class group
D) Reading and defining words that have ambiguous meanings

**10**

As part of an evaluation, a special education teacher brings his high school student with an intellectual disability to the nearest supermarket and asks him to find and buy a good.

Which of the following is the teacher's assessment type?

A) Interview
B) Authentic
C) Ecological
D) Portfolio

**11**

What is a special education teacher's best response to Carla who has a learning disability regarding her excessively detailed notes?

A) Show Carla how to use a more telegraphic style when she takes notes.
B) Provide Carla with index cards to limit the amount of space available for taking notes.
C) Remind Carla that she can use a photocopier for sections of a source that requires extensive notetaking.
D) Teach Carla how to use text headings to focus her notetaking on key concepts.

**12**

Stephen struggles with retaining information about any lesson. Which strategy could best benefit Stephen?

A) Note-taking
B) Self-regulation strategies
C) Mnemonic strategies
D) Time management skills

**13**

Which of the following refers to the use of a student's classwork as a means in evaluating the progress and adapting of the instructions?

A) Curriculum-based assessment
B) Guided practice
C) Summative assessment
D) Standardized achievement testing

**14**

Mr. Smith wants to assess his son's recreation and leisure skills. Which of the following is the best method for Mr. Smith to evaluate his son with visual impairment?

A) A checklist from the expanded core
B) A classroom visit
C) An evaluation by a trained specialist in visual disabilities
D) A conversation with a school counselor

**15**

Which of the following statements regarding transitions for students with special needs at age three is TRUE?

A) A transition planning meeting must happen before the end of June during the year the child turns three.
B) The parents/guardians of a child who is eligible for special education services are required to obtain such services for their child.
C) The child's family/caregivers should make decisions regarding the child's services and family support.
D) Discussion of options and the transition process would be done in a planned meeting that will take place in the year after the child's third birthday.

CONTINUE ▶

**16**

It is important that a special education teacher has a good communication with student's parents or guardians to facilitate productive and harmonious education.

At a parent-teacher conference, which of the following will give them good relation?

A) The special education teacher conducts the conference using education jargon and technical language.
B) The special education teacher instructs the parents on how to provide guidance to the student in a more consistent manner.
C) The special education teacher sets the agenda and ensures that the student's parents adhere to the discussion points.
D) The special education teacher discusses the student's academic strengths and offers suggestions for how the student can improve on weaknesses.

**17**

What strategy would most effectively meet the goal of a special education teacher regarding the development of the student's self-confidence for a more prosperous transition from high school to college?

A) Pairing each student with a successful adult mentor who has a similar disability who can serve as a positive role model
B) Assigning each student to research a particular career and present oral report about it
C) Having each student interview several adults to obtain information about the positive and negative aspects of each person's job
D) Encouraging students to have a part-time job for after school

**18**

A speech-generating communication device used by a 5-year-old with Down syndrome and associated language delays provides spoken words and related sounds when the child touches a picture on the screen.

Which of the following is the most important benefit of this device for the child's future learning?

A) It would support her acquisition of vocabulary and concepts.
B) It would help extend the length of her attention span.
C) It would promote her problem-solving skills.
D) It would improve her understanding of print concepts.

**19**

What strategy would best meet a special education teacher's goal involving the increase of the student's participation in different types of leisure activities?

A) Having students conduct a survey to determine the types of leisure activities in which their same age peers most commonly participate
B) Inviting guest speakers from various school clubs and extracurricular activity groups to present information to the students
C) Assigning students to research various types of leisure activities and having them each present the information to the class
D) Integrating time into the weekly schedule on a consistent basis for students to participate in various types of leisure activities

**20**

Which of the following is an advantage of using drill-and-practice software to reinforce the mathematical computation skills of a student with a learning disability?

A) Direct comparisons with different students' performances
B) Virtually unlimited examples of any given type of problem
C) Immediate feedback on answers
D) Highly entertaining visual displays

**21**

A new fourth-grade teacher sends a letter to her students containing a list of classroom supplies the student will need as well as personal information such as why she enjoys teaching, her recent summer experiences.

Which of the following is the greatest benefit of the teacher's actions?

A) It provides a way for the teacher to encourage students to reflect on their summer activities.
B) It provides a way for the teacher to foster positive rapport with the students.
C) It provides a way for the teacher to give students an idea of the teacher's expectations.
D) It provides a way for the teacher to ensure the students will be prepared for the upcoming school year.

**22**

Melissa, a high school student with a disability, is enrolled in the district's vocational training program. She is assigned to an activity that measures the speed and accuracy of sorting and classifying skills.

Which of the following would classify Melissa's activity?

A) Adaptive behavior checklist
B) Performance-based assessment
C) Criterion-referenced test
D) Personal interest inventory

**23**

Ms. Peterson noticed that one student in her 3rd-grade SDC class has not made any progress in reading.

Which steps should Ms. Peterson do next to improve this student's reading skill?

A) Recommend the student to receive more restrictive services
B) Inform the student's parents that the student is at risk of failing
C) Set a more realistic goal for the student to achieve
D) Adjust the lessons to the student's needs and monitor her progress every two weeks

**24**

In teaching a culturally diverse class, which of the following is the most important?

A) To research the students' backgrounds to determine their cultural learning styles
B) To emphasize teaching your own cultural backgrounds because it's easier to do
C) To punish students who discriminate other students with different cultures
D) To provide a culturally neutral learning environment

**25**

How might the RSP teacher of Samantha, a third grade RSP student who struggles with reading comprehension, advise her Gen-ed teacher to differentiate her instruction?

A) Give Samantha extra reading assignments to do at home.
B) Give Samantha extra writing assignments to do in the classroom.
C) Front load vocabulary with her before the reading assignment.
D) Discuss Samantha's learning profile and guide the teacher in developing strategies that suit her individualized needs.

**26**

Which of the following should an elementary school teacher of students with mild intellectual disabilities do to assess a student's ability to correctly sound out letters and words to newspaper reading?

A) Select articles from the local newspaper for students to read
B) Develop writing exercises using words from the curriculum
C) Prepare worksheet exercises based on single sentences from newspaper articles
D) Prepare teacher-made newspaper articles for the students to read

**27**

Two teachers are co-teaching a math class, where both of them are providing instruction to the class as a whole. What model does this situation represent?

A) Parallel teaching
B) Alternative teaching
C) Team teaching
D) Lesson study teaching

**28**

Which of the following is the implication of "appropriate education" as courts have determined by such cases as Hudson v. Rowley (1982)?

A) Learners with disabilities will have the same achievement opportunities as peers.
B) Interpreters will be provided for all deaf children.
C) Services that maximize achievement will be provided as long as the cost is not prohibitive.
D) Students will have all the resources and related services needed to fulfill their potential.

**29**

What could a middle school teacher do to the intellectually disabled students to assess their ability to correctly sound out letters and/or words on reading newspaper?

A) Prepare worksheet exercises based on single sentences from newspaper articles
B) Develop writing exercises using words from the curriculum
C) Select articles from the local newspaper for students to read
D) Prepare teacher-made newspaper articles for the students to read

**30**

A 9th-grade student was diagnosed with a Specific Learning Disability in abstract reasoning, and also struggles with executive functioning. Based on the student's condition, what writing unit would be appropriate?

A) Using a graphic organizer, have the student write a 3-paragraph argumentative essay.
B) Have the student dictate a 3-paragraph argumentative essay to a scribe.
C) Have the student write a paragraph with a clear topic sentence, supporting details, and transitions between sentences.
D) Have the student write a 5-paragraph argumentative essay on a given topic.

**31**

Which of the following statements shows the primary goal of a special education teacher when setting up a meeting with a new fourth-grade teacher who has a student with ADHD in his class?

A) To direct the teacher to resources with background information about the student's disability.
B) To help the teacher understand the accommodations specified for the student.
C) To establish procedures for monitoring the teacher's compliance with the implementation of the student's accommodation.
D) To discuss when the student's parents should be contacted regarding the child's behavior.

**32**

An eighth-grade student with specific learning disability receives direct reading instruction in decoding skills to improve word recognition of vocabulary words.

Which of the following does the instruction represent?

A) A metacognitive strategy
B) A compensatory approach
C) Scripted reading instruction
D) A remedial approach

**33**

What procedure should the teacher follow in ensuring nonbiased assessment results in the evaluation of the academic achievement of a student who is an English language learner?

A) Using a variety of formal and informal assessment instruments to collect information.
B) Administering assessment instruments beginning at a lower grade level.
C) Administering informal assessment instruments to the students in a familiar location.
D) Relying primarily on standardized nonverbal assessment instruments.

**34**

Ms. Samson is a new ESE teacher for middle school students. She wants to learn more about instructional practices.

Which of the following could she use as the most reliable source while searching on the Internet?

A) An address ending in .gov or .org
B) An online message board for educators
C) A Web site ending in .com
D) A frequently updated educational blog

**35**

Gina is a student with learning disability in writing. Which of the following would be best for English language arts (ELA) teacher to improve Gina on punctuation under the special education teacher's guidance?

A) Sending Gina to the resource room to review final drafts for punctuation errors before submitting her work
B) Setting a short period of time aside each day for Gina to work on punctuation exercises
C) Holding Gina accountable for punctuation errors when grading her work, as articulated in the IEP
D) Having Gina and a classmate exchange final drafts and correct each other's punctuation errors

**36**

Carla, a new middle school student, has cerebral palsy and associated speech impairment. Her teacher wants to determine the most effective way for her to participate in class discussions so she consults with a special educator.

Which of the following could be the special educator's suggested approach?

A) Position Carla in the center of the classroom so that everyone can hear her contributions.
B) Give Carla five minutes to prepare a response to a question during discussions.
C) Ask Carla questions at the very beginning of discussions to minimize her anxiety.
D) Discuss with Carla her preferred method of communication.

**37**

Ms. Roberts set rules on her students that she will give tally marks for every followed instruction and deduct tally marks for every broken instruction. She then observes a decrease in the number of students breaking the rules.

Which of the following would losing tally marks for breaking class rules represent?

A) Token economy
B) Antiseptic bouncing
C) Positive reinforcement
D) Response cost

**38**

A 3rd-grade pupil with ADHD performs slightly below grade level and has a low concentration threshold.

Which test taking accommodation would be most appropriate for this pupil?

A) Providing short breaks throughout the test
B) Providing a test booklet where the pupil can directly answer the test
C) Providing a test that has larger fonts and colorful illustrations
D) Providing a shorter test

**39**

Which of the following is an example of an intervention that would help Paul, a student diagnosed with autism and is in an inclusion classroom, to participate in a paired activity?

A) Pair him with another student diagnosed with autism.
B) Provide a scaffold-ed guided approach using images and pictures.
C) Have him use a word processing device to assist with communication.
D) Pull him from all group activities.

**40**

A special education teacher meets with parents of a prekindergarten student with developmental delays to support her learning at home.

Which of the following teacher recommendations given is likely to have the most significant long-term impact on a child's literacy development?

A) Use flashcards to provide her with practice recognizing the letters of the alphabet
B) Give her various types of drawing and coloring activities to help develop her creativity
C) Help her learn how to write her name and the names of other family members
D) Read aloud a variety of children's fiction and nonfiction books to her on a regular basis

**41**

Which of the following should teachers ensure role-playing and practice activities do to provide effective social skills instructions to elementary school students with disabilities?

A) These activities should be entirely improvised by the students without teacher input.
B) These activities should be age appropriate and relevant to students' lives.
C) These activities should directly acknowledge the effects of students' disabilities.
D) These activities should introduce mnemonics designed to help students recall social conventions.

**42**

**Response cost** is a procedure in which a specific amount of available reinforces is contingently withdrawn following a response in an attempt to decrease behavior.

Which of the following purposes would response cost suit well as an intervention?

A) Decreasing excessive competitiveness among students
B) Decreasing the incidence of angry outbursts
C) Increasing the speed of performance in mathematics
D) Improving students' understanding of directions

**43**

Due to a second-grade student's inability to recall the letters of the alphabet in sequential order as well as an inability to make letter-sound associations, the student is referred for a comprehensive individual evaluation.

Which of the following should the team first consider when selecting assessment instruments to include in the student's evaluation?

A) The assessment instrument's ability to produce data relevant to the student's educational needs.
B) The assessment instrument's ability to provide a baseline for measuring the student's future progress.
C) The assessment instrument's ability measure the student's development across multiple domains.
D) The assessment instrument's ability to be modified to accommodate the student's disability.

**44**

Judith, a 12th-grade student with autism, has poor social skills despite her having consistent passing grades.

Which intervention could most benefit Judith to develop her social skills?

A) Providing her with material scaffolding supports
B) Enrolling her in a functional curriculum
C) Providing her with a supplemental curriculum
D) Providing her with task scaffolding activities

**45**

A transferee student was observed to be needing occupational therapy services. If you were the teacher of this student, what should you do to ensure the services are being implemented?

A) Recommend to discontinue the service in the student's IEP
B) Provide the services in the school
C) Recommend to parents to refer the student to an occupational therapist
D) Contact the school's Occupational Therapist to let them know the student requires services

**46**

The students with mild autism in a certain 3-5 SDC class start to misbehave every time the lesson changes.

If you were the teacher of this class, what would you do to help the lesson transitioning go smoother?

A) Place a countdown timer on the wall to make everyone aware when is the transitioning time.
B) Reward students who transition well and punish those who don't.
C) Discuss one lesson only per day so that no transitioning will be needed.
D) Post a visual agenda that reflects the daily routine.

**47**

To monitor a students' writing skills progress, a teacher sets a goal of "writing a 5 sentence paragraph".

Which action below would most appropriate support this goal?

A) Evaluate the students' writing skills progress twice a year
B) Assess the students' writing skills daily
C) Evaluate the students' writing skills progress every six weeks
D) Assess the students' writing skills once a year

48. What strategy would be most effective for a special education teacher and a general education teacher to use in promoting positive interactions between students during the first day of school?

A) Creating questions for students to use in interviewing each other to find out specific information, then having students share the results of these interviews with the class.

B) Asking each student to bring in a favorite family photograph to post on a classroom bulletin board.

C) Pairing students who are known to be quiet with students who are known to be more outgoing to work together on various tasks and play together at recess.

D) Assigning students to write a paragraph about their likes and dislikes to read aloud to the class.

## SECTION 6

| # | Answer | Topic | Subtopic | # | Answer | Topic | Subtopic | # | Answer | Topic | Subtopic | # | Answer | Topic | Subtopic |
|---|---|---|---|---|---|---|---|---|---|---|---|---|---|---|---|
| 1 | D | TB | S2 | 13 | A | TB | S2 | 25 | D | TB | S2 | 37 | D | TB | S2 |
| 2 | B | TB | S2 | 14 | A | TB | S2 | 26 | A | TB | S2 | 38 | A | TB | S2 |
| 3 | C | TB | S2 | 15 | C | TB | S1 | 27 | C | TB | S1 | 39 | B | TB | S2 |
| 4 | B | TB | S2 | 16 | D | TB | S1 | 28 | A | TB | S2 | 40 | D | TB | S1 |
| 5 | C | TB | S2 | 17 | A | TB | S2 | 29 | C | TB | S2 | 41 | B | TB | S2 |
| 6 | C | TB | S1 | 18 | A | TB | S2 | 30 | A | TB | S2 | 42 | B | TB | S2 |
| 7 | C | TB | S2 | 19 | D | TB | S2 | 31 | B | TB | S1 | 43 | B | TB | S2 |
| 8 | A | TB | S2 | 20 | C | TB | S2 | 32 | D | TB | S2 | 44 | B | TB | S2 |
| 9 | B | TB | S2 | 21 | B | TB | S2 | 33 | A | TB | S2 | 45 | D | TB | S2 |
| 10 | B | TB | S2 | 22 | B | TB | S2 | 34 | A | TB | S2 | 46 | D | TB | S2 |
| 11 | D | TB | S1 | 23 | D | TB | S2 | 35 | C | TB | S1 | 47 | C | TB | S2 |
| 12 | C | TB | S2 | 24 | A | TB | S2 | 36 | D | TB | S2 | 48 | A | TB | S2 |

## Topics & Subtopics

| Code | Description |
|---|---|
| SB1 | Collaboration & Communication |
| SB2 | Instructional Strategies |

| Code | Description |
|---|---|
| TB | Learning Environment |

Made in the USA
Monee, IL
11 July 2021